The Spirit of Hula

Photos and Stories from Around the World

Shari 'Iolani Floyd Berinobis

BESS PRESS

3565 Harding Avenue
Honolulu, Hawai'i 96816
phone: (808) 734-7159
fax: (808) 732-3627
e-mail: sales@besspress.com
http://www.besspress.com

Design: Carol Colbath
Lei border photographs courtesy of Hide Kalanimoku, Kohala Company
Photos pages 84–85 courtesy of Dave Filler Stillwater Photography
Photos pages 92–93 courtesy of Lisa Byrne Photography
Photos page 102 courtesy of Kai Uahinui
Photo page 103 courtesy of Northwest Hula Studio

Library of Congress Cataloging-in-Publication Data

Berinobis, Shari Iolani Floyd.
  The spirit of hula : photos and
stories from around the world /
Shari Iolani Floyd Berinobis.
    p. cm.
  Includes illustrations, glossary.
  ISBN 1-57306-223-5
  1. Hula (Dance). I. Title.
GV1796.H8.B47 2004   793.3-dc21

Glossary definitions are taken in part from Mary Kawena Pukui and Samuel H.
Elbert, *Hawaiian Dictionary,* rev. and enl. ed. (Honolulu: University of Hawaiʻi
Press, 1986).

Mele.com was a primary source for obtaining contact information for the *hālau*
that were invited to appear in this book.

Photo page 116 © Thérèse Ann
Photo page 117, top, © Svetlan
Photo page 117, bottom left, © Anne S. Ditmeyer
Photo page 117, bottom right, © Arnaud Ville

08 07 06 05 04   5 4 3 2 1

Printed in Korea

To my parents, Allene and Chick Floyd, my husband, Tito, and
our daughters, Tiana and Shaylene

Contents

Hawai'i

U.S. Mainland

International

My Journey Through Hula

Many who do not know me have asked, "Who is she to author this book?" My answer to you is, "My *'uhane kia'i* came to me in a dream. I am simply a vehicle chosen by God, or the higher spirit, to present and share the beauty of the dance, humbly and with deep respect." This book is presented to you from deep within my heart and soul, out of love for Hawai'i, her people, her culture and traditions. It is not meant to differentiate or discriminate in any way, but to embrace the beauty of the hula as it is known and felt in Hawai'i and throughout the world.

Showcased are but a handful of the many magnificent *hālau* performing today. Their *kumu hula*, teachers, and directors have different levels of knowledge, different levels of protecting and honoring their love of the Hawaiian culture. *Kumu* and *haumāna* who were born into the world of hula have been blessed with a rare and wonderful gift. Others, far from Hawai'i or without family support, have struggled to obtain instruction and knowledge.

Their love and desire have persevered, and today, they dance with pride.

On this journey through the world of hula, those I have talked with were open, proud, and gracious about sharing their *mana'o*. I was awed by the sincere nurturing they give, especially to our *keiki*.

For many I have spoken to, hula is all about being Hawaiian. For others it is about feeling the spirit of Hawai'i deep within the soul and upholding her culture and traditions. For some, it is about feeling lost and reaching out to that which brings them closer to feelings of completeness. It is about respect and love for our heritage, our *kūpuna*, the *'āina,* and one another. It is about giving unselfishly and unconditionally and finding peace within.

It is with deep respect, gratitude and honor that we recognize all the treasured *kumu hula*, the beautiful souls who have passed through our lives. They have left a precious legacy that we must *mālama*, preserve and protect. *Mahalo nui loa* for taking the journeys, for giving life to hula

through your remarkable, creative spirits, for taking the time to envision the dance on different levels, allowing creativity to flow freely while keeping the spiritual importance, heritage, and traditions first and foremost. Your gifts will be treasured and held steadfast in our hearts forever.

I have been so very blessed, and thank all of the magnificent *kumu hula,* directors, and instructors who gave me the opportunity to take this journey, enabling me to renew old acquaintances, to *ho'oponopono* with others, and to create closer bonds of friendship and aloha. *Mahalo nui loa* for opening your hearts, for trusting me and for sharing your *mana'o* so graciously.

Acknowledgments

I am so fortunate to have Bess Press working with me on this project. My deepest gratitude to the entire staff, especially publisher Ben "Buddy" Bess, editor Revé Shapard, and designer Carol Colbath.

My deepest aloha

To guests Kawaikapu Hewett, Blossom Kunewa, Uncle George Holokai, and Hide Kalanimoku for sharing their selfless, creative *manaʻo*, for taking the time and offering their special aloha; the many *kumu*, instructors and directors, for filling these pages with incomparable beauty, warmth, and aloha; Robert Cazimero, whose belief in me and in the purpose of this book made this project become a reality.

A special mahalo

To Blaine Kia for his endless support, for being a sounding board through many frustrating moments, and for the joy of his friendship; *kaʻu kumu,* Millie Kawaa, and friends Ilima Dela Cruz and Ainsley Halemanu, for the many hours they spent making sure my *ʻōlelo* Hawaiʻi was *pono;* Hide Kalanimoku, for his *kōkua* in obtaining the information and beautiful photos from the Japan *hālau;* my *hānai* daughters, Angela Ginoza and Allie Tamanaha, for working with me on the glossary and brightening many days.

My heartfelt gratitude

To others who helped make this book possible, including Christie Adams, Maureen Andrade, Cheryl Burghardt, Jenner Charles Cauton, Vanessa Christner, Julie Inada, Diane Gietzen-Jett, Chris Justino, Robbie Kaholokula, Erin O'Kelley, Kaleo Kia, Yvonne Lopes King, Tomoko Kumagai, Cyril Lacaniellier, Wendy Mays, Denise Moreland, Nani Naʻope, Chris Punahele, Kamai Punahele, Mapuana Ringler, Aubrey Tamanaha, and Arnaud Ville.

To many of my dearest, supporting friends, who worked with me through this journey, Iris Asao, Hula Cauton, Barbara Chang, Sue, Bob, and Melissa Green, Julie James, David Kauahikaua, Marci Keller, and Annette Peterson, for computer and Internet assistance, pickup and delivery from one end of the island to the other, being there when I needed a shoulder and a few glasses of wine, and most especially for their precious gifts of love and friendship.

Aloha wau iā ʻoe

To my beautiful family: Tito and Mom "Tudie," for rallying through this project with me, giving me space when I needed quiet time, and seeing me through to its completion; Mom and Dad Eye, for just loving me and always being there when we needed them; Tiana and Shaylene, my lovely daughters, for e-mail assistance and giving great massages and for just being who they are. Thanks to them all, for understanding and being there for one another when I was inaccessible. Their gentle spirits and never-ending love have given me great comfort and endless happiness.

Hula: Harmony of the Head, Heart, and Hands

For the sixty-eight *hālau* featured in this book, hula is not just about memorizing hand and foot movements or learning the meaning of a particular song or using various implements. Hula begins with respect: for the ancestors and the conception of the dance, respect for *nā kumu*, who bring great knowledge, strength, and aloha to their *haumāna*, and respect for ourselves.

Hula—on the U.S. mainland, in other countries throughout the world, as well as in Hawai'i—then becomes all about being Hawaiian, thinking Hawaiian, or feeling Hawaiian, and going deep inside to reach the rich culture and heritage that has been shared. It is about feeling the dance with every pore, cell, muscle, and heartbeat. It is bringing all of this together while surrendering the spirit to create the inner balance, the inner dance.

You will find this message as you read here about people and practices important to each *hālau*:

Kumu Hula

Kumu hula here means "hula teacher." In practice, it usually means those who have been through a formal *'ūniki* ceremony.

Ke Po'o

Ke po'o here means "leader" or "director." Out of respect to Hawaiian tradition, many hula teachers choose not to call themselves *kumu hula*.

Kū'auhau

Kū'auhau here means "lineage." These are the mentors, or those who have inspired the *kumu* and *ke po'o* to dance and to teach.

Nā Lālā

Nā lālā here means "branch," or "limb." These are the members of the *hālau*, many of whom travel long distances to learn not just hula, but the culture and customs of Hawai'i.

Akeakamai

Akeakamai here means "lover of wisdom, philosopher." These are the beliefs, often rooted in Hawaiian proverbs and teachings, that inspire the *kumu* and directors and unite the *hālau* in a common goal.

Mana'o Pūlama

Mana'o pūlama here means "cherished memories." These are special events or performances, including travel to share hula with other cultures.

Ho'okō 'Ana

Ho'okō 'ana here means "performance, achievement." These are milestones in the lives of the *kumu* and in the history of the *hālau*.

Guests

The lessons of hula enter through our heads, pass through our hearts, and go out through our hands. It is the unity of thoughts, words, feelings, and actions that brings about the glorious harmony of the head, heart, and hands. The four guest authors whose stories follow illustrate this. Beloved *kūpuna* Blossom Kunewa and George Holokai describe what hula has meant to them; Kumu Hula Kawaikapuokalani Hewett writes about the interrelatedness of spirituality, healing, and hula; and Hide Kalanimoku, whose beautiful leis are found throughout the book, shares what the lei means to him.

George Ainsley Kananiokeakua Holokai

"Hula is a universal communication of life filled with the Aloha Spirit for the world to embrace."

I studied hula under Kumu Hula Tom Hiona, in the early 1950s. When we were living in Papakōlea with my mother, Tom woke all of us up early one morning. He said, "Come on, we're going to the studio. I want to be in the studio before the sun rises." My mother,

my cousin, Tom, and I rushed to the studio and sat down in a circle. Tom started praying and chanting. My mother asked him, "What are you doing?" He said, "I just gave George a special *'ūniki*. I know George can carry on my work at the studio. One of these days I'm going to walk out of the studio and you'll never see me again." Afterwards, we left Tom at the studio— and I never saw him again. He just disappeared.

It wasn't until five years later that I found out from one of my students that he had passed away.

After I took over the studio, I had to carry on and do the many different jobs Tom had done. Because I was young, I was afraid to face the public. When we performed, during the *kahiko* numbers I would sit behind the curtain and chant. During the *hula 'auana* numbers, of course, I had the musicians with me, and I would have them go out front. I would hide in the back, and they would nudge me and say, "Go on, go on out." I would say, "No, no," because I was too ashamed.

Since I was only in my twenties I

thought I needed to learn more. I began studying hula under Lillian Maka'ena, a relative of Auntie 'Iolani Luahine's. She said that before she met me, she saw me in a dream. A week later her husband told her that he had the same dream and described me to her. One night he and some friends went down to the original Don the Beachcomber's in the front of the International Market Place and saw me dancing. He went home and told Maka'ena, "I've found the boy in our dreams."

In 1952, I got a call from the Aloha Week office asking me to be a court chanter. I didn't know if I could do it, but Mama—that's what I called Maka'ena—said, "Boy, you call them back and say 'yes.' I've been teaching you all these chants and you are ready! You call them back and tell them you accept." So I did.

One day they called me and told me, "George, tomorrow we need you. You are going to be christening a canoe." I panicked and called Mama right away. She said, "Kanani, don't worry, I will give you a chant for

christening. When you do the blessing, don't use salt water, because people handle the water and salt when it is being processed, and it's not pure. You tell them you want a coconut."

I asked, "Why a coconut?"

She said, "Because the coconut water has never been touched by man. It's pure. You cut off the top and use the liquid to bless."

Even now, whenever I do a blessing, I use the coconut water, and if there's any left over, I dig a hole and pour the rest into the hole. I never leave the coconut behind or throw it away there, but I take it home so no one can pick it up.

Over the years I have had the opportunity to judge many hula competitions. When I was first asked to judge the Merrie Monarch Festival in Hilo, it was held in the armory, not in the arena as it is today, and there was no stage.

The night of the competition, Dottie told us, "Judges, I want you to make two lines facing each other and take turns chanting." I asked, "What are we going to chant?" She said, "You'll be bringing the court in." That was the only year they asked the judges to chant the court in. I really think they should bring that back. It was so nice, each of us taking turns.

I remember one year in the fifties they had a mass of chanters at the *ho'olaule'a* in Waikīkī. They lined us up in three or four rows, with the Aloha Week Court behind us. There again, we all took turns chanting as the court paraded behind us down Kalākaua Avenue. There were so many of us; it was beautiful!

I gave up teaching at the studio in the late 50s. I was working in Alfred Apaka's show in Kaiser's Hawaiian Village Tapa Room. I was also teaching all day in the studio. The doctor told me I was working too hard and had to give up one or the other. I decided it would be the studio.

For many years I taught hula for the City and County of Honolulu's Department of Parks and Recreation. I've conducted countless hula workshops with the Hawai'i State Foundation on Culture and the Arts and the Kalihi-Pālama Culture and Arts Programs, and in many mainland cities.

Today, I give weekly classes to fellow *kumu hula* and instructors who seek to further their knowledge. It began a couple of years ago when my friend Laverne asked me to start a class. She gathered some people together, and the mother of one of my friends opened her house in ʻĀlewa Heights for us to use. Laverne said she didn't know who would show up, but for me to just be ready to teach. So I arrived and waited for some kids to show up. All of a sudden, Kauʻi Kamanaʻo walked in, Leialoha Amina walked in, and I turned to Laverne and said, "Laverne, these are not *haumāna*, these are *kumu hula*!" Pretty soon we had an entire group of *kumu* and *alakaʻi* in the house.

Later on, someone asked, "Kumu, do you teach implements?" So I began teaching implements. We began with the *ʻulī ʻulī*, and some didn't even know how to rattle! I told them they had to rattle properly or it would throw off the beat. After they learned a song, we moved on to the *pūʻili,* and they said, "Oh Uncle, your dances are hard!" I really have so much fun with them. We have over thirty in the class now and they're still coming.

When I teach beginners, I believe they have to learn to dance with feeling from within, not from the outside. It's not just the motions. I tell them to look at the words and the translations to the song and really feel what the song is saying—express themselves, from the eyes and smile. Sometime I watch a *hālau* perform and they are just doing the motions that their *kumu* taught them. They don't dance with feeling. When you feel the dance, the people in the audience are going to feel you.

Many will say I'm too picky when I judge. That's the way I was taught. Sometimes in competition dancers are wearing a lei and they don't pay attention to it. It may not be the lei the song is talking about, but they should at least lift the lei when it's mentioned—admire the lei, or at least acknowledge its fragrance from the lei to the nose. Sometimes they go overboard with flowers and I have to laugh. I look at the pretty faces of the dancers, so small and sweet and then there's this big, giant bouquet on the side of their face that is just monstrous! Don't go overboard. Keep it small. Keep it simple.

Today, so many *kumu* have so many motions for things. A flower is a flower and the scent comes from the flower, not from the outside. And when they are talking about a person, it's from the head down, not way up there. The person is not a giant. Even when you're making motions of the lei, it's just over your head. Sometimes I see it coming from the heavens, and I think, "Oh no!"

Keep it simple, keep it from within, and always, keep dancing.

Blossom Keliʻiʻaukai Joshua Kunewa

I started dancing professionally at the age of fifteen. During World War II, my sister Lorraine and I performed for the military around the island, dancing and bringing smiles to the faces of soldiers. We went to the mountains, to the ocean, to foxholes, anywhere we were able to lift morale.

It was frightening to me to hear the sounds of the soldiers as they marched by our house, night after night. Our mother, however, heard music in the beats of the boots as they hit the ground, and as she listened, she turned the awful sounds into a beautiful *mele* and dance. The first two verses were *mele*, and the third verse only drumbeats, the drumbeats of the soldiers passing by.

I began teaching hula in 1956 at the Military Mānana Housing. I taught only *hula ʻauana* and some instrument dances. I never learned to dance true *kahiko*. My father forbid us dancing it or even watching it. To him there were too many sacrifices symbolized in the dance. We learned quickly to be good listeners and tried to memorize what we were allowed to watch. If he knew what the story was about, and it told of things relating to the *ʻāina* or the heavenly spirit, we were allowed to watch. He was a devout Christian and was very strict. His belief was so strong that he even changed his last name from Kahele to Joshua.

In later years, Lorraine and I learned a little *kahiko* from Henry Pa and Tom Hiona, who taught us the beautiful chants that Daddy approved of. I loved the pig dance and wanted to learn it, but it, too, was taboo.

In 1963 Lorraine and I left Hawaiʻi with our husbands to go to Europe to share the Hawaiian culture and bring hula to the other side of the world. In Germany we put together a great show using the available military children, teenagers, and adults. My agent, Mel Slate, booked six shows for us in Berlin and another six in Spain.

While we were still in Germany, Pan American Airlines invited me to be part of their performing group called the Hawaiian Club. I soon became the entertainment director, and we traveled to Holland, France, and Italy. When we returned to Berlin, we were asked to perform for Green Week, a very prestigious event. It was such an honor to represent Hawaiʻi and share our love of hula. During our performance people kept calling out, "Hawaiʻi, Hawaiʻi, Hawaiʻi!"

In Germany we couldn't get ti leaves, so we had to use green raffia to make our costumes. We also had to use imitation flowers or the occasional fresh flower we could find along the streets. When we did luaus in the summers, Pan American sent orchids and plumeria flowers and leis. We found everything we needed to prepare the food, including *'opihi* that we brought in from the seashores of France. We had to make powdered poi, but it tasted just as good as the real thing. We mixed it, cooked it, and put it on ice. We found everything except luau leaves. The pig, the salmon—everything there—was inexpensive.

I loved Europe. I didn't really miss home, because we always knew we were coming back. I could have stayed another ten years, but the Vietnam War started so we were forced to leave. During the Vietnam War we were on tour in Missouri doing shows at the NCO Club and in private clubs in the area. Every week we'd lose more and more musicians as they were recruited to go overseas. We'd have to call home for musicians every week and never knew who would be playing for us. Many of these talented people were lost in the war.

In 1969 we returned home and were immediately asked to go to Japan to open the Mikazuki Hotel in Kataura

Chiba. I took an entire cast of musicians, dancers, and singers to perform there for three months. When I came home we joined Hawaiian Airlines and went on promotional tours over the next three years. When that stint was finished, Sally Edwards, who was with Theo H. Davies, asked me to do shows for all the large ships that came into port on O'ahu. I performed with Auntie Genoa Keawe, Leina'ala Cypriano, Nora Santos, Arthur Lyman, Wendell Silva, and Annie Hu.

I've been the entertainment director for the Queen Ka'ahumanu Society since 1987. We enjoy perpetuating the Hawaiian culture and performing whenever we are available.

In 1997, my sister and I began lecturing at the University of Hawai'i. I spoke and taught *hula 'auana* there for five years. The first teacher they had was 'Iolani Luahine. What an honor to follow in her footsteps.

I always enjoyed sharing a story about a time when I went to a retreat in Kapo'o in Hilo with Reverend Kaina. While he was talking to the students, he told them, "You're going to the university here, you're learning the Hawaiian language, and you think you

know it all through learning. No, you don't. Just because you get a degree, you don't know everything. Your real true language comes from your *kūpuna nui*, your great-grandparents. Those are your real teachers, the ones who speak the language."

How true it is! Our parents spoke fluent Hawaiian, but in those days it was *kapu*. It was never taught in school and couldn't even be spoken at home. Anyone caught speaking Hawaiian language was punished. My parents used it only while they were teaching. Now, at my age, trying to

learn it is very difficult. I understand more than I can speak. Lorraine went back to school and got her degree in Hawaiian. She is now the expert in the family when it comes to Hawaiian history and language. If you are lucky enough to come from a home where the Hawaiian language is spoken, embrace it and use it.

My mother was a great inspiration. Lorraine and I are carrying on her legacy—her style, her moves and interpretations—by passing it on to the children.

Hula is now spreading throughout the world. I think it enriches hula to be appreciated around the world, and hula enriches the lives of those it touches. Many people who left Hawai'i, military children or those who were born away from Hawai'i, never learned to dance. Now they miss Hawai'i, and learning hula shows their love for Hawai'i.

When I was young, a gentleman who later became a family friend opened a nightclub in Mexico. He was dating a local girl, Shirley, from Hawai'i and fell very much in love with her. Evidently, she eventually took off and he couldn't find her. He missed Shirley so much he decided to open a nightclub, calling it The Maunaloa. He wanted to keep it Hawaiian because of his deep love for her. So he hired dancers from Hawai'i and contacted my mother, asking her to train them. At the time it was the only Hawaiian nightspot in Mexico.

I'm invited to judge many hula competitions. When people ask me for hula advice, I always say, "Take everything you do seriously and, most important, believe in yourself. Learn from your *kūpuna*, obtain more background about the *mele* and dance, be creative and have your own image."

Spirituality, Healing, and Hula
Kawaikapuokalani Hewett

The first time I saw Kawaikapu, I knew there was something special, very deep and meaningful about him. He carried the essence of royalty in the way he walked and moved. I was drawn by his spirit and knew I wanted to meet him. So I took a deep breath, walked up to him, and introduced myself. The moment was brief, but I walked away knowing there was more

to this man than what most people could see.

Many years later, sitting with him in the Flamingo Restaurant in Kāneʻohe, I knew that my feelings were right on the mark. As we sat there talking, I learned that his lineage went all the way back to the kings and queens of Europe from his grandfather on his mother's side. He is descended from King Ferdinand and Queen Isabel of Spain, King Louis of France, and King Edward of England. He also inherited an entire Hawaiian genealogy from his father's side, which includes their own ancestral kumulipo. *He has spent many years working with Kawena Johnson researching their* kumulipo *in its entirety.*

For me, spirituality, healing, and hula go hand in hand. You cannot have one without the other. My students will all tell you that they're learning spirituality from me because of who I am and how I teach. Prayer is incorporated each time we meet. My mannerisms

reflect my capacity for healing, and I'm always the peacemaker. Harmony is important to healing, harmony is important to tradition. My students will always say that I never criticize. It's not my *kuleana*. My *kuleana* is to maintain my *pono*, my goodness. My relationship with my ancestors is more important to me than standing as a critic for others. I just have this look on my face and my students know exactly how I feel about issues. That is in alignment with the tradition of ʻ*ike*, which is knowledge. If you have an ʻ*ike*, you have a thought implanted through the spiritual world into your thought. That's the best way to describe ʻ*ike*. That ʻ*ike* comes from the ʻ*aumakua,* and that ʻ*ike* is the spiritual link. By maintaining your *pono*, your goodness, you're able to maintain ʻ*ike*. ʻ*Ike* is also sight, your eyes, your *maka,* and your ability to see, whether you see through this dimension or have the ability to see through a spiritual dimension. My students watch me, because the ʻ*ike* in my eyes lets them know exactly what they need to do.

For me, the best way to teach is to "be." Words mean absolutely nothing if you cannot be. Being is the best way to impress and to nurture your students. You cannot teach one thing and be another. It doesn't work. Sooner or later they'll be able to see through it, but if you are exactly what you teach, that will come across very clearly and they'll get it.

It's really important to me to touch the lives of my students. And I know that, once I've touched them, sooner or later they will become a large part of me; in five years, ten years, fifteen years, twenty years—eventually, they will become like me. And I look forward to that. I want to be around to see that happen. I hope to live to be 100, and if I'm lucky enough, to 110! And if I am that lucky, I will enjoy watching them develop and pass on what I have shared. I look forward to seeing that in my children, I look forward to seeing that in my grandchildren, and I look forward to seeing that in my great-grandchildren. And when I speak of that, I speak of all my children, which includes every single one of my students. They don't come in as *haumāna*; they come in as my children.

It is a characteristic of my family that we are able to communicate with the spirit world. I depend on my Auntie Momi, who does readings, to guide me spiritually. One day she said to me, "Kawaikapu, when you walked into this house, behind you walked all these kings and queens and not just Hawaiians, but Europeans beautifully dressed and wearing crowns." I smiled at her knowingly, and said, "That's nice Auntie."

I'm lucky, because at age 50 I'm still young. Auntie Momi says that at age 50, I'm ready. At 50, I tell her, "No, I'm still learning. I want to learn. There are so many things I need to learn." And she asks, "When will you be ready?" I don't have an answer for her. She just smiles and says, "Just go with the flow." So, I do.

People often refer to me as an enigma because I do hula and I do healing. They always ask me, "Are you a hula dancer or are you a healer?" Hula and healing are not two separate things; they're actually closely related. The tradition of hula and the tradition of healing in our culture are two very, very important, ancient traditions.

Another time, the question was posed to me a bit differently: "What are you? Are you a *kumu hula* or are you a healer?" My response was, "I'm a healer because I'm a *kumu hula*, and I'm a *kumu hula* because I'm a healer." It goes back to an ancient legend, and this is the legend of the goddess Keaomelemele, one of the hula goddesses. She also studied healing traditions. This is the tradition of my *kumu*, Auntie Emma DeFries, an exponent of the hula and the *oli*. Auntie Emma studied with Kaleohaʻalulu Napahi, and she studied chanting with Kaleo Kaʻaluli Napaʻi. Her grandfather also taught her the traditions of healing at a *heiau* in ʻAiea. This is the same *heiau* that she took me to, sharing the tradition of healing. Hiʻiakaʻikapoliʻopele, the youngest sister of Pele, was also a hula dancer and healer, whose tradition came from Hōpoe. One day she brought Lōhiʻau back to life, which confirmed her ability as a healer. She was also a great chanter and *haku mele* who composed many beautiful *mele*.

The healing tradition with hula must be a very compassionate, yet wise one. The way my students receive the healing tradition from me is through my mentoring. There is no other way that I can enter into the process. It is not that I say to them, "Today, we're going to have a lesson in healing." I never have to say anything, for every aspect of my life has to reflect that, so that they see it's real. That lesson is life and that's how I work with them. I'm very proud when I hear that they are going to a school of social work, to a school of medicine, to a school of psychology, or to a school of law. If along the way we help someone access their success through wellness, that follows right in the line of our tradition of hula.

Being a *kumu hula* who was trained as a *kahuna,* by a *kahuna,* I am now called upon to work within the perimeters of western medicine as consultant on particular cases in hospitals. People may not know this, but I've already made great leaps and bounds in the area of medicine. Having that opportunity to be listed as a consultant is a big thing for me, and a great honor.

My spirituality, my healing, and my hula are every part of who I am and what I am.

Lei Making in Japan
Hide Kalanimoku, Aoyama, Japan

In the Pan Pacific region, many customs involve leis. However, I believe Hawai'i makes the best use of the lei. I have a special attachment to the Hawaiian lei, and it has been the foundation upon which I have based my life.

The lei is a necessary part of hula. These days, many dancers use imitation leis. This is the result of industrialization, which ignores the spirit of hula. I believe fresh flowers and greens should be used. This is especially important for the Japanese. Since we are from a different culture, we should take care to honor and respect the sacredness of the hula. For this reason I began incorporating fresh flowers and greens for leis and hair ornaments. At a market in Japan I can find flowers such as roses, freesia, hydrangea, and orchids.

The first time I put on a lei was on the Island of Hawai'i, when my teacher, Robert Cazimero, made one of *palapalai*, ginger, and *'a'ali'i*. What was astonishing was that we picked the materials as we walked along the path, and as we sat on a bench, with the sound of 'Akaka Falls in the background, Robert made the lei in an instant!

Occasionally, I bring back or order flowers and greenery from Hawai'i, such as ginger, *lehua, liko,* and *pala-palai* and *pala'ā* ferns.

When I am making leis, Hawaiian music plays in the background, and my heart is in Hawai'i. I become so absorbed in making a lei, thinking only of the person who will be wearing it, that I forget the passing of time. This is my way of life. I would like to hand down the joy of making leis to the next generation, to share with others the Hawaiian culture.

Hawai'i

Hālau Hula Ka No'eau

Based in Kamuela, on the Island of Hawai'i, we have performed around the world for the past seventeen years.

Kumu Hula
Michael Pili Pang

Kū'auhau

While maintaining our cultural integrity, we preserve the unique dance styling of Hula Master Mai'iki Aiu Lake's *hula ku'i*. I would like to thank each of my elders for guiding and inspiring me to live up to the title of *kumu hula*.

Nā Lālā

Our *haumāna* are strongly encouraged to use their individual knowledge, skills, and creativity as ways to build self-esteem, community pride, and social identity within their hearts and minds. Performances and educational activities that promote cultural understanding, preservation, and innovation provide an excellent opportunity for understanding and honoring our Hawaiian heritage and the traditions of Hawai'i's people. In addition, our *haumāna* have knowledge of hula's beginnings—that it evolved from a religious service where poetry and pantomime took the form of dramatic art.

Akeakamai

It is our mission to promote and sustain the inherent cultural and artistic values of Hawaiian dance. It is our vision to someday see Hawaiian dance viewed as a world-class art form. We believe that hula is best represented as a lei; we encourage everyone to appreciate the beauty of each blossom, the fragrance and love that this symbolic expression of aloha represents. We are so proud to be a part of the perpetuation of this great culture.

Mana'o Pūlama

We began the first three months of the new millennium visiting three countries and twelve states, performing for more than thirty thousand people.

Ho'okō 'Ana

Our *hālau* has grown and become what it is today because of the love and commitment of our students, performers, communities, and the other organizations we service. They are the backbone of our success and the lifeline that keeps us striving to reach the goals of education, presentation, tradition, culture, and preservation.

Hālau Hula Ka Ua Kini Maka Lehua ʻO Hawaiʻi

Based on the Island of Hawaiʻi, we have shared our culture and our history with many places throughout the world.

Ke Poʻo

Brandon Kamuela Himalaya was born into a *hālau ʻohana* and was taught from birth that hula was to be his way of life.

Kūʻauhau

My grandparents, Margaret and Samuel Bishaw, taught me the importance of carrying on their legacy and upholding and respecting the history and culture of Hawaiʻi. Today, I continue gathering knowledge through Kumu Hula Francis Henry Pokukaina Keanaʻaina and look forward to experiencing a formal *ʻūniki*.

Nā Lālā

The love, sorrows, triumphs, and losses of our ancestors are beautifully relived through each dancer's inner interpretation of the hula. It is our connection to who we are and what brought us to this point. There are many ways to preserve one's culture, but none as moving and emotional as that which is given through our dance of hula. I try to instill this belief in members of my *hālau*. I also encourage my *haumāna* to embrace knowledge sent from any direction, as it is a lifelong, never-ending joy.

Akeakamai

Hula is Hawaiʻi and Hawaiʻi is hula; they are one in the same. For me, hula is a way for our ancestors to communicate with our *keiki*, enabling them to learn of the significance of days past. It is a way for our *keiki* to carry on their great legacy and make a difference in the world today.

Anyone can dance, but a true dancer tells a story that takes the audience through the journeys of the past, present, and future as if they were actually there.

Hoʻokō ʻAna

We have traveled to New Zealand and several times to Japan as part of a cultural exchange program. Because of their deep love of hula, many *keiki* who had never left Hawaiʻi or even visited the other islands have traveled to these countries. Such experiences allow the *keiki* to not only share their culture and experiences, but also learn about different lifestyles, cultures, and histories of those far away. This is a great educational opportunity for *nā haumāna*, as I strongly believe that education is the key to our past and our future.

Hālau Hula Ka Ua Kini Maka Lehua 'O Hawai'i

Hālau Hula 'O Hokulani

O'ahu

Nā Kumu Hula
Larry and Hokulani DeRego

Kū'auhau

The roots of our *hālau* go back to the 1880s and the royal court of Prince Jonah Kalaniana'ole Kūhiō, where Annie Kaleikaulana Ka'ihe was a court dancer. The hula continued in 1913 when Annie gave birth to Blossom Kailiponi Clark, who became a hula dancer in San Francisco's old Barbary Coast Tahitian Hut. While dancing in the 1930s and 1940s, Kailiponi also began teaching; she continued to do both for the next fifty years. She was recognized as a Living Treasure of Hawai'i. Kailiponi is Larry's mother and Hokulani's *kumu hula*.

Nā Lālā

We established Hālau Hula 'O Hokulani in 1985 to share the art of hula and the Hawaiian culture with all children and their families. We encourage closer relationships by teaching Hawaiian values and developing opportunities for families to work and play together in mutual harmony and respect.

Through hula our dancers learn history, language, and arts and crafts. Every year we test them to determine whether they are ready to move up to a higher level. They are tested not only in dancing and *oli*, but also in making leis, playing the ukulele and other instruments, discussing Hawaiian history and its culture, and respecting others. Students select a time in Hawaiian history, person of royalty, or related subject and compile a report with pictures or drawings.

Akeakamai

We are dedicated to instilling the love of our Hawaiian heritage in our students through hula. We also believe that dancing skills are drastically improved and enhanced through active participation in performances and competitions.

Mana'o Pūlama

Each year is filled with *'ohana* activities that include an Easter potluck, several May Day performances, a Hawaiian studies summer program, the Moanikeala Hula Festival at the Polynesian Cultural Center, hula camp at the Queen Lili'uokalani Children's Center, participation in the Aloha Week festivities, and performances at various fundraisers.

Ho'okō 'Ana

We travel extensively throughout the year to learn about various places and customs. During one trip, our students had the opportunity to teach a group of Native Americans about the art of *lauhala* weaving. This was a unique experience, enabling the students to share our special aloha spirit and a bit of our Hawaiian culture.

Hālau Hula ʻO Hokulani

Hālau Hula O Kawaili'ulā

Kailua, O'ahu

Kumu Hula

Chinky Māhoe has been dancing hula since 1967. He currently travels throughout the continental United States and Japan to conduct hula workshops and perform in concerts with the Mākaha Sons.

Kū'auhau

Māhoe began dancing under hula master Uncle George Nā'ope. Ten years later Māhoe joined The Men of Waimāpuna under the direction of the late *kumu hula* Darrell Lupenui, who gave his blessing and helped Māhoe begin Hālau Hula O Kawaili'ulā in 1979.

Nā Lālā

Kawaili'ulā, which means "mirage of shimmering water," is a family name as well as Māhoe's middle name. In 1981, the *hālau* entered its first hula competition, a high school contest sponsored by the Queen Lili'uokalani Children's Trust. When the young men won first place, interest and enrollment in the *hālau* grew quickly.

The *hālau's* initial purpose was to enter competitions. The group entered and won numerous hula competitions, such as the Keiki Hula Competition, Kamehameha Hula Competition, and Merrie Monarch Festival, before traveling the world and performing in Japan (Sapporo, Osaka, Hiroshima, Kyoto, Okayama, and Tokyo), the United States (Portland, Seattle, Tacoma, San Francisco, Los Angeles, Washington, D.C., Maryland, and New York), Canada, New Zealand, Okinawa, and Korea.

Akeakamai

The focus of the *hālau* is to perpetuate the hula and Hawaiian culture by conducting hula workshops and performing all over the world.

Ho'okō 'Ana

After spending two years traveling, the *hālau* returned to the Merrie Monarch Festival in 1993 and won first place in the overall men's division for the next five years. The men of Kawaili'ulā placed first in the men's overall division eight times, and second or third overall six times. The women of Kawaili'ulā placed first in the *hula kahiko* in 1994 and second overall in 1995.

From 1994 to 1996, the young boys of the *hālau* took first place in all categories, including overall division, at the Keiki Hula Competition. In 1997, they placed first in all categories except the *hula kahiko*, in which they placed third.

In addition to traveling to London, England, in June 2004, the *hālau* is planning a trip to Sweden for the World Christians Gathering of Indigenous People, held each time in a different country.

H̄ālau Hula O Kawaili'ulā

Hālau Hula ʻO Namakahulali

East Honolulu, Oʻahu

Kumu Hula
Shirley Kanemura Recca has been dancing since she was nine years old.

Kūʻauhau
Puanani Alama, my first hula teacher, represents the time when hula became a way of life for me. In the 1960s, my sister, Manu Kanemura Bently, recommended that I replace her as the featured hula stylist in Martin Denny's show at the Kahala Hilton Hotel. Marty, who is now world-renowned, was like a second father to me while we performed together throughout the mainland.

In the late 1970s, Marian Jay offered me my first taste of teaching hula during a summer program held at Punahou. In my early years as a *kumu hula*, Aunty Joan Lindsey encouraged and supported me whenever times got rough and I felt like giving up.

My mother-in-law, Lei Bright Recca, has been instrumental in expanding my knowledge of hula and *mele*. I learn more from her old-style performances than I could from anything printed in even the best books.

Others who have enriched my life and art are Maddy Lam, Alice Namakelua, Irmgard Aluli, Sol Kekipi Bright ("Uncle Mona"), Ed Kenny, Bev Noa, Nina Kealiʻiwahamana, Mahi Beamer, Alex McAnges, Leo Anderson Akana, Patricia Lei Anderson Murray, Robert and Roland Cazimero. My husband, Joseph Kekipa Bright Recca, happens to have one of the most beautiful voices to ever come out of Hawaiʻi. He and I have had many wonderful years with Tihati and Cha Thompson of Tihati Productions and their gifted performers.

Mahalo ke Akua for this wonderful journey and my beautiful *ʻohana*, my husband, our daughters, Elan Hemakanamakamaimaikalani and Delys Hulalimaikalanimai, and our grandson, Andrew Kekipi Kazuichi.

Nā Lālā
It is an honor and pleasure to teach all that I have learned of our heritage through the art of hula. I wish for the style of hula I share with my *haumāna* to be pleasing to the eye and spirit of the beholder. My joy comes from witnessing a student loving what has been shared and seeing the perpetuation of our culture carried on with pride. I hope what I teach is *pono* and useful to my *haumāna*.

Akeakamai
Hula communicates life experiences and thoughts of *wā kahiko* and *kēia manawa* through storytelling from one's soul. I believe the hulas from the past must be kept as pure as possible.

Manaʻo Pūlama
I am so thankful to have danced with gifted performers such as Charles K. L. Davis, ʻIolani Luahine, Kaʻupena Wong, Leilani Sharpe Mendes, Benny Kalama, Barney Isaacs, Buddy Hew Len, Sonny Kamahele, Kalani Fernandes, Violet Pahu Lilikoʻi, and countless others. How fortunate I am to have worked with and known these treasures.

Hālau Hula 'O Namakahulali

Hālau Hula 'O Nāpunaheleonāpua

Based in both the Kāne'ohe and Kalihi areas of O'ahu, we have been dancing since July 1993.

Kumu Hula
Rich Pedrina

Kū'auhau
As a former dancer of Hālau Hula 'O Kawaili'ulā, under the auspices of Chinky Mahoe, for twelve years, Rich was a participant and a recipient of many awards at the Merrie Monarch Festival. He also continually enriches his knowledge of the dance through his studies of the spiritual and classic styles of old Hawai'i through his classes with Kimo Alama-Keaulana and George Holokai, old-time hula masters, *kumu hula*, and entertainers.

Nā Lālā
We have dancers from all walks of life, between the ages of three and seventy-seven. What makes our *hālau* unique is that it embraces everyone. Regardless of shape, size, or previous knowledge, everyone with the desire to learn can be taught the hula. Even individuals with virtually no hula experience can be trained, guided, and inspired to become accomplished, competition-level dancers. Our students learn the basic movements systematically; gradually these movements became natural for the body. When dancers are instructed in the various motions to the songs and chants, their hands and feet already know what to do.

Akeakamai
The *hālau* motto is "It doesn't matter who you are, or where you come from, for as long as you have the love for hula, you belong here."

Mana'o Pūlama
The dancers' disciplined execution of exact movements in unison provides the audience with a breathtaking experience. The energy exhibited by all of our dancers is transferred to spectators, and after each performance fans are usually asking for more.

Ho'okō 'Ana
We have dancers who are enjoying the dance even though they are physically challenged.

Hālau Hula 'O Nāpunaheleonāpua

Hālau Hula 'O Pohai Kealoha

Based in Honolulu, we have entertained throughout the world for over thirty-three years.

Kumu Hula

Kealoha Kalama has been a well-known entertainer, recording artist, and producer for the past forty years. In addition to producing her own Polynesian review for some of the best Waikīkī showrooms, she has judged many hula competitions in Hawai'i, California, Mexico, Washington, and Japan.

Kū'auhau

Many people have played an important role in my hula career, including John Pi'ilani Watkins, Uncle Joseph Kahaulelio, Vickie I'i Rodrigues, Bill Ali'iloa Lincoln, Lena Machado, and my mother, Virginia Kalama. Our biggest *hālau* supporter is my husband, Wilfred Thomas Cabral, who has given me never-ending love and patience.

It is so important to recognize and thank those who have supported, loved, and been a special part of our growing *hālau. Mahalo nui loa* to Mama Genoa Keawe, Leina'ala Haile, Ainsley Halemanu, and Kawaikapu Hewett, and to Amy Hanaiali'i Gilliom for her wonderful talent, personality, and beauty. To Myra English, Peter Ahia, Arthur Hew Len, and Kekua and Kalani Fernandez: Though you have passed on, you are always in our *pu'uwai*. And to all of my cherished *'ohana, haumāna*, and *hoaloha*: *Aloha wau 'ia 'oe*.

Nā Lālā

We are not a "traditional" *hālau*. We travel all over the world, sharing Hawai'i and the aloha spirit with such places as Las Vegas, Japan, and Europe. We have also performed in Hong Kong, Singapore, Thailand, Korea, Australia, New Zealand, Fiji, Tahiti, Johnson Isle, Guam, Kwajalein, Canada, and across the United States.

We are actually on the road so much that we don't have time for annual traditional events. But no matter where we are performing, we always do *pule* before each show.

Hālau Hula ʻO Pohai Kealoha

Hālau Kaleihulumamo

Island of Hawai'i

Kumu Hula
Poni Kamau'u

Kū'auhau

My life has always been immersed in everything Hawaiian. I spent many years at the knees of Auntie 'Iolani Luahine while she was a curator at Hulihe'e Palace in Kona, Hawai'i, and the Royal Mausoleum in Nu'uanu, O'ahu. When I was very young, she shared with me her dream of starting a *hālau* in her Nāpo'opo'o home. She wanted it to be a place where both children and adults could learn about hula and the Hawaiian culture.

Nā Lālā

Hālau Kaleihulumamo was created as a testimony to Auntie 'Io's belief that hula is truly a gift from heaven that entices its dancers to learn more about the hula arts and share their knowledge with others. I named the *hālau* after my great-great-grandmother Kaleihulumamo O Hi'iaka i ka poli O Pele, who was the eldest sister of Keahi Luahine, a court dancer in the time of King Kalākaua. I honor her with this name so that we may be able to carry on the beautiful legacy that was passed down through generations.

We have nearly one hundred *haumāna*, who are placed into various groups. While I prefer smaller groups, I enjoy working with the larger groups on a daily basis. We travel occasionally, taking private journeys that are primarily related to protocol events.

Akeakamai

Hula is like a breath of life that is exquisitely embodied and expressed in patterns of movements and sound. It is everything that makes up the universe. Hula is a vital expression of our Hawaiian culture and is performed throughout the world. The *pahu*, *ipu heke*, chants, and language of hula all inspire us to a deeper understanding of the heritage and traditions of the Hawaiian people.

Ho'okō 'Ana

Hālau Kaleihulumamo joins together with other *hālau* to help perpetuate a proud family legacy descending from *kahuna nui*, court chanters, and court dancers of the Kalākaua era.

Hālau Kaleihulumamo

Hālau Ka Liko ʻO Kapalai

Oʻahu

Kumu Hula

Ainsley Keliʻi Halemanu believes he was destined to perpetuate the Hawaiian culture, language, and hula with a deeper and better understanding, love, and appreciation.

Kūʻauhau

I am eternally grateful to my parents, family, friends, and those who have long passed on for bestowing upon and blessing me with their heritage and wisdom. Because of them, I commit to do the same for every person I cross paths with, as they may not have been as fortunate as I have been. My mentors remind me that I am not alone in this quest.

Nā Lālā

I offer my knowledge to the children unconditionally and share it with the world. This great gift of knowledge, which was part of my everyday life and so often taken for granted, was unknowingly the steppingstone that would pave the way to my future.

I teach my *hālau* that hula is the source, the *piko*, the link to everything that surrounds us in our everyday lives. As we embrace this lifestyle, we must take time, as our elders did, to stop and listen to the wind and see how it makes the palm trees sway. In hula we feel the rhythm and many moods of the ocean.

Did our forefathers so cleverly weave the multitude of knowledge into the hula so that it would survive in the Western way of life and prosper in this new millennium? I believe so, as many of our hula songs and chants, *oli i mele*, reveal proverbs, historical information, poetry, migration stories, and creation tales. This great wealth of knowledge is endless, and I share it with my *haumāna*.

Akeakamai

E pōʻai nā kamaliʻi i ka hula, ua honi aku noʻeau lākou e nā kāpuna (teach the children the hula and they will be embraced with the knowledge of our ancestors). May the heavens and our *nā kūpuna* smile and bless us with the spirit of aloha in the deeds we undertake and in our everyday lives.

Hālau Ka Liko 'O Kapalai

Hālau Kawaianuhealehua

Mānoa, Oʻahu, and Maui

Ke Poʻo

Colsen "Ina" Kaluawaipakui Kanei credits Robert Cazimero, Wayne Chang, and Hālau Nā Kamalei with first awakening his interest in dancing hula. Up until then, he had been only an interested onlooker, anxiously awaiting the beating of the drums, seeing the excitement on the dancers' faces, and hearing the joyous comments of the happy audiences. When he was sixteen years old, Colsen began dancing with Kahaʻi Topolinski.

Kūʻauhau

As a high school senior, I danced with Michael Dela Cruz and Na ʻŌpio O Koʻolau. Michael was really strict with his Polynesian dancing, but under his tutelage I was able to dance in Japan, Taiwan, and other places throughout the world.

In 1985, I joined Chinky Māhoe and his Hālau Hula O Kawailiʻulā to compete in the Merrie Monarch Festival. It was the pride I felt while dancing that kept me in the *hālau* for eleven years. Chinky stressed endurance and strength; everyone in his *hālau* walked away with "hula legs." I owe my competitive attitude and showmanship to the years I spent dancing with Chinky.

In 1998, I joined the Papa Kumu Hula class in Waimānalo with Kumu Kawaikapuokalani Hewett. Since then, he has been my *kumu*, grounding force, spiritual guide, and inspiration.

Nā Lālā

In September 1997, with Chinky's blessing, I opened my *hālau*. Kumu Kawaikapuokalani Hewett blessed and named us Hālau Kawaianuhealehua. Just as it was passed down to me, I want nā *kāne*, *kūpuna*, *wāhine*, and *keiki* of Hālau Kawaianuhealehua to experience everything hula has to offer in knowledge, pride, and glory.

Akeakamai

Commitment is essential in dancing hula and entering competitions. Most important in hula is upholding the respect of our ancestors, remembering who we are and where we've come from, and never giving up when things get tough.

Hālau Kawaianuhealehua

Hālau Ka Waikahe Lani Malie and Hālau Kahulaliwai

In 1997 we opened our *hālau* bases on the islands of Kauaʻi and Oʻahu (see pages 22 and 23), in Sacramento and Antioch, California, in Montana (see page 84), and in Chiba, Japan (see photos, page 21). We now nurture other schools in Stockton, parts of Southern California, and Japan.

Kumu Hula
Blaine Kamalani Kia

Kūʻauhau
In 1999, I decided to learn the power and wisdom of the *hula pahu*. A master wood carver, Etua Tehauri, allowed me to be his apprentice and learn the skill, the *loea*. After several months of training and learning, I single-handedly made four *pahu* drums. As my *hālau* leaders aspire to new levels within the hula rankings, I award them a drum made from my hands so they will know how much I appreciate their sacrifice and dedication year after year, and how proud I am of them. I have awarded seven drums. I dream of awarding many more in the near future.

Nā Lālā
All of our institutions throughout the world hold annual *hōʻike* celebrations. The main purpose is to give back to the families and to the communities in order to make people aware of who and what we are and what we do. We work endlessly to perpetuate Hawaiian values. When people see our *hōʻike* they see that we are not just a cultural dance group but a family united with love, humility, and strength. We have a family of over 1,200 students.

I started a *papa kumu* (teaching class) and a *papa alakaʻi* (leadership class) to foster our teachings at all levels. I travel every year in a constant rotation to nurture and support my leaders.

Akeakamai
We embrace the concepts of hula, family, religion, and labor. We work hard and unselfishly to instill these qualities by setting examples for all. Hawaiian traditional practices are the lifeline to our existence and the sustenance of our culture.

Manaʻo Pūlama
In addition to our *hōʻike* celebrations, we regularly perform for professional, commercial, and private affairs.

Hoʻokō ʻAna
The growth and development of my top leaders, Cristy Laʻamea Almeida on Kauaʻi, Dale Kupono Sugiki on Oʻahu, Juni Kalahikiola Romuar in California (teaching 200 students per week), Rika Haliʻipua Asano in Japan, and Macy Massey in Montana, are the biggest accomplishments ever!

Hālau Ka Waikahe Lani Malie and Hālau Kahulaliwai

*T*he Ladies of Hālau Ka Waikahe Lani Malie

Po'opua'a

Cristy La'amea Almeida, who began studying under Kamalani in 1997, is the highest-ranking student he has ever had—the only achiever of the title *po'opua'a* (head pig). La'amea uses the natural beauty and resources of Kaua'i to instruct, give ambience to performances, and enrich the traditional spiritual growth of the students.

The Men of Hālau Kahulaliwai

Kōkua Kumu/Hoʻopaʻa

Dale Kupono Sugiki has been with Kamalani for ten years. His dedication and sacrifice are unmatched, and he is highly respected by the entire institution and body of *haumāna*.

Other Oʻahu leaders, who train one hundred students each week, include Kamalani's wife, Kaleonani Kia, Tamra Leilani Porter, Dean Kualono Dantsuka, Trisha Kawauʻi Kodama, and Leinytte Kahaʻi Rosco.

Hālau Ke Kiaʻi A ʻO Hula

Based in Kapālama, Oʻahu, this *hālau* has participated in hula festivals in Hawaiʻi and the continental United States for the past twelve years.

Kumu Hula

Kapiʻolani Haʻo, pictured on the left, has been dancing *hula* since she could walk and always to the delight of her *kūpuna* and *mākua* (grandparents, parents, aunts, and uncles). She first danced on the Merrie Monarch stage when she was eighteen years old.

Kūʻauhau

In 1979, Kumu Kapiʻolani completed her *hula* training from Master Kumu Hula George L. Naʻope and graduated to Kumu Hula Palapala. Since then she has also had the opportunity to learn from Kumu Hula Kamuela Naeʻole, Kumu Hula Kawaikapuokalani Hewett, and Kumu Hula George Holokai.

Nā Lālā

Kumu Kapiʻolani enjoys sharing both ancient and modern *hula* with students of all ages. Children, parents, and grandparents often attend classes together, making hula, literally, a family affair. Even Kumu Kapiʻolani's own grandsons and two-year-old grandniece join in when they can. This special feeling of *ʻohana* makes Hālau Ke Kiaʻi A O Hula, which means "the guardians/keepers of the dance," so unique. The *hālau* is much more than a place to just teach or learn a dance.

All *hālau* experiences are considered to be once-in-a-lifetime. Kumu Kapiʻolani strives to provide as many *haumāna* as possible with opportunities to travel to different places and learn about different cultures.

Akeakamai

One of the *ʻōlelo noʻeau* Kumu Kapiʻolani believes in and passes on to her *haumāna* is *ʻAʻohe pau ka ʻike i ka hālau hoʻokahi,* which means "Not all knowledge lies in one school."

Manaʻo Pūlama

The *hālau* has performed at the King David Kalākaua Hula Festival in Kona, the E Hoʻi Mai Ka Hula Piko World Invitational Hula Festival in Waikīkī, and the Kau I Ka Hano Hula Festival in Las Vegas. The *hālau* has also enjoyed participating in cultural festivals with the Ainu, the indigenous people of Japan, in Hokkaido, Tokyo, and Osaka.

Hoʻokō ʻAna

For the past five years, the *hālau* has been honored with invitations to participate in Hawaiʻi's most prestigious hula competition, the Merrie Monarch Festival in Hilo.

Hālau Ke Kiaʻi A ʻO Hula

Hālau Mohala O Ka Pua Hau Hele

Kaua'i

Kumu Hula
Puamohala Kaholokula

Kū'auhau

Noted *kumu* such as Uncle Joseph Kahaulelio, Ku'ulei Punua, and Ed Collier have had a profound impact on Puamohala's education as a young hula student. Roselle Keli'ihonipua Bailey continued by teaching her a more serious study of this art form. Puamohala met Robbie Kaholokula, son of famed *haku mele* James Kalei Kaholokula, and the young couple unified their talents to create Na K Productions and built a modest legacy of entertainment and hula. Hālau Mohala O Ka Pua Hau Hele, or "the bud of the crawling *hau*," was the name given by Puamohala's father-in-law, their mentor and most profound critic. The senior Kaholokula, known for such Hawaiian music classics as "Pua Olena," "Nane," "Kikau," and "Ke Ahi Wela," would guide Robbie and Puamohala through the business of music and performance.

Nā Lālā

A new twist has been the addition of Praise Hula classes. Puamohala has performed *hula 'auana* in church for years.

Akeakamai

Kumu Bailey taught us that hula was much more than coming to class and learning motions to songs or ancient chants. Hula is a way of life, a study in a culture and a proper respect thereof. God has blessed us with privilege to learn from our teachers before us. This blessing continues when we pass that knowledge to others in the best way that we know how, with excellence, compassion, and humility.

Mana'o Pūlama

Puamohala was the featured dancer with Na Kaholokula, Robbie's band. The band headlined the showrooms of the Sheraton Coconut Beach Hotel, Aston Kaua'i Resort, Sheraton Kaua'i, and Outrigger Kaua'i Beach Resort. It was from Pua's *hālau* that a professional dance team, The Kaleinani Dancers, was formed. "Those were good times, and great memories. I sometimes miss the showroom performances," recalls Puamohala in a moment that offers just a hint of reflective history.

Robbie and Puamohala also are raising their children in the business. Their oldest son, Baron, grew up watching them perform and already plays several instruments and has a band at school. Daughter Lei U'i loves to sing and dance the hula and often helps mom teach the younger children of the *hālau*. As a family, the Kaholokulas perform at home in Hawai'i and have been invited to Japan several times.

Hālau Mohala O Ka Pua Hau Hele

Hālau Nā Kamalei

O'ahu

Kumu Hula
Robert Uluwehi Cazimero, known for the past twenty-four years for his modern, unconventional, and creative styling, believes that a good *kumu hula* acts as counselor, teacher, mother, father, friend, and sibling.

Kū'auhau
People who have made a difference in the quality of my life and the *hālau* are my *kumu*, Ma'iki Aiu Lake, and mentors such as Maynard "Gramps" Ho'apili and Loyal Garner.

Ma'iki was honest with me. Though she was not always happy with what I did, her support was steadfast. Her passing made me appreciate the importance of the heritage and tradition of her hula styling—the art of Hawai'i and dance, expressing everything we hear, see, smell, taste, touch, and feel.

Nā Lālā
My dancers are special and they make me believe I'm a good teacher. The youngest students are seventeen years old; the oldest make up the support system that nourishes the new guys. Together we become a light at the end of the tunnel and clear paths to see one another through difficult times, while teaching life, tradition, honor, and respect. Being able to honestly say, "I know what you're going through. I've been there, too," is truly remarkable.

Akeakamai
Hula is no longer just about glitz and avant-garde display: It's about life. What we learn in hula helps us through the basics of life and our individual paths. Turning negatives into positives is what hula and life are all about for

me. It is the way I think, the way I teach, the way I work with my students, and what I believe is paramount for the gentlemen of Hālau Nā Kamalei. It's a real challenge, but so exciting and worthwhile.

Mana'o Pūlama
When the lights come up, it's not the dancers who are on the line, but the teacher. The success of a performance brings with it quality, tradition, and respect. We feel an overwhelming and amazing amount of pride when we put on a good show. Watching my dancers makes me so happy—they are magical.

Performances also give us opportunities to honor great teachers and students. I purposefully and honorably respect my students for their trust in me.

Ho'okō 'Ana
We have traveled the world, performing in venues such as the Miss America Pageant, in Carnegie Hall in Boston with the unbelievably talented Boston Pops, and at the Waikīkī Shell.

*H*ālau Nā Kamalei

Iwalani School of Dance

O'ahu

Kumu Hula

Iwalani Wahinekapu E. R. Walsh Tseu feels blessed to have been born and raised on an island steeped in abundant beauty and rich in cultural heritage. For her, hula is not just a dance, but an art and lifestyle that should reflect one's inner beauty, grace, and humility. She lives by the belief of preserving, perpetuating, and promoting the hula.

As a cultural resource, Iwalani is frequently called upon to share her *mana'o* with various organizations. She has shared the gift of hula with the world as an Ambassador of Aloha. She is listed in *Nāna I Nā Loea Hula,* a book of living *kumu hula* treasures, and in *Who's Who: Best Teachers of America 2000*. She is also the recipient of numerous awards and letters of appreciation for outstanding talent and community services.

Nā Lālā

Established in 1974, we are not a competitive *hālau*, but a school of dance that learns as much as we can from the many ethnic cultures represented in Hawai'i. To teach hula is to touch a life, because I teach out of love. I teach my *haumāna* to share the beauty of hula within our community, yet I recognize that competition is positive because it forces the student to research hula's origins and purpose, achieve a deeper understanding of the dance, and ultimately bring it to its highest expression.

Through the discipline, practice, study, and experience of hula, my *haumāna* learn core values of compassion, responsibility, loyalty, and integrity.

Akeakamai

By applying a "look, listen, learn, love, and live" approach to hula, my *haumāna* gain a better understanding of the dance and of how to ultimately connect to the world.

Hula translates the symbols of words into movement and meaning and is the combination of emotion, thought, expression, passion, and language. It's an outer expression of what Hawaiians call *mana* (our own divine power). Through hula, we communicate all there is about our world and everyday lives. To dance hula in its deepest form, we must be receptive to the value it has to offer.

Hula is healthy and healing. It embraces the physical, mental, emotional, and spiritual aspects of our beings. It tones our minds, as well as our bodies, and often causes feelings of joy and happiness. Hula truly is poetry in motion.

Iwalani School of Dance

Keali'ika'apunihonua Ke'ena A 'O Hula

Based on O'ahu, this school of hula has entertained the world for twenty years.

Kumu Hula

Leimomi Ho says her life has been and will always be centered on hula and the love of sharing her talent with others.

Kū'auhau

This school of hula perpetuates the traditional hula styling and legacy of Victoria Keali'ika'apunihonua I'i Rodrigues (Aunty Vicky), an accomplished composer, musician, entertainer, and teacher who greatly influenced the world of hula and Hawaiian music.

Leimomi was raised as a *punahele* along with Aunty Vicky's own children.

Music and hula were an inherent part of their family life. Many years later, it was at Aunty Vicky's insistence that Leimomi opened the doors of her own hula school. Aunty Vicky gave the use of her Hawaiian name, Keali'ika'apunihonua, which means "the chief who traveled around the world." She forbade the use of the word "*hālau*" and chose the word *ke'ena* (studio or place to gather) instead. She asked that no advertising be done, believing that those students who came to Leimomi's doors came out of their desire to learn hula. Leimomi promised to keep the traditional dances she learned from hula masters such as Lokalia Montgomery.

In addition to Aunty Vicky, Leimomi's mentors include Aunty Kekau'ilani "Nana" Kalama, who took Leimomi under her wing and began officiating over formal ceremonies as *kumu hula* after Aunty Vicky's death, and Aunty Kamamalu Klein.

Nā Lālā

The symbols of this hula school and what they represent are an introductory part of each student's learning. The blossoms of the school are three yellow roses, Aunty Vicky's favorite flowers, which represent the Holy Trinity. Leimomi instills within each member of her *ke'ena* the importance of respecting the art of hula and the cultural traditions passed down by the *kūpuna*.

Akeakamai

This school strives toward being of one heart, one thought, and one love, so that the goodness of life may always be perpetuated.

Ho'okō 'Ana

This hula school has enjoyed many years of blessing in its activities and competitions. True to the name Keali'ika'apunihonua, Leimomi and her students have traveled to and performed in the outer islands, Japan, the continental United States, and Tahiti.

Aunty Vicky

Keali'ika'apunihonua Ke'ena A 'O Hula

Kuhai Hālau O Kawaikapuokalani Pa ʻOlapa Kahiko

Established in 1978, this *hālau* is based in Heʻeia on the beautiful windward coast of Oʻahu.

Kumu Hula

Kawaikapuokalani Hewett, renowned singer, composer, and practitioner of traditional Hawaiian healing, has been teaching hula for the past thirty-two years. Now fifty years old, he feels that life is just beginning: "I have raised three children and now I am helping to raise three grandchildren. It is my love for my grandchildren that keeps me performing. I want to be a role model for them as long as I can and inspire them to follow in my footsteps."

Kūʻauhau

Growing up, Kawaikapuokalani was blessed to have received specialized training from his grandmother, Eve Kanaʻe. While attending the University of Hawaiʻi at Hilo, he studied under Edith Kanakaʻole, a distinguished *kumu hula* and composer. Kawaikapuokalani has also had an illustrious array of teachers and mentors, such as the memorable ʻIolani Luahine and Kahuna Aunty Emma de Fries. Over the years, he has been recognized as Aunty Emma's protégé for his extensive knowledge and use of traditional Hawaiian healing methods.

Nā Lālā

Kawaikapuokalani's *haumāna* hail from all parts of Oʻahu, Kauaʻi, Maui, and Japan. Many are working toward their *ʻūniki*, or formal hula graduations, with hopes of someday becoming teachers who will carry on the traditions that have been passed down to them.

Manaʻo Pūlama

Kawaikapuokalani has had the distinct pleasure of dancing with many well-known entertainers, including Aunty Genoa Keawe, Palani Vaughn, the Lim family, the Peter Moon Band, and many others. For nearly twenty-six years, he has performed with Jerry Santos, Haunani Apoliona, and Olomana on Saturday nights in the Paradise Lounge at the Hilton Hawaiian Village Hotel in Waikīkī.

In addition, he frequently travels with his *hālau* to Japan to put on special concerts, perform at dinner parties for dignitaries, and give workshops in *hula ʻauana* and *hula kahiko*. He has also been featured in many magazines and television specials in Japan.

Hoʻokō ʻAna

Kawaikapuokalani has received recognition for his musical compositions from the Hawaiʻi Academy of Recording Artists and won countless Nā Hōkū Hanohano Awards, including awards in the Single of the Year, Most Promising Artist, *Haku Mele*, and Hawaiian Album of the Year categories. His award-winning compositions include "Poliʻahu," "Kawailehua," "Kapilina," and "Aloha Kuʻu Home A I Keʻalohi."

𝒦uhai Hālau O Kawaikapuokalani Pa ʻOlapa Kahiko

Magic Hula Studio

O'ahu

Kumu Hula

Lorraine Kaheamalani Kahele Joshua Daniel and Blossom Keli'i'aukai Joshua Kunewa

Kū'auhau

We learned hula from some of the greatest *kumu hula* of all time, such as Mary Ho, Henry Pa, and Tommy Iona. However, the greatest influence and most rewarding teachings came from our late mother, Rose Joshua, proprietor of the Magic Hula Studio. It was through her love, wisdom, guidance, and humility that we learned to truly appreciate and embrace the art of hula. We learned at an early age that hula was not to be used strictly for monetary gain, but more importantly for what we could share and give to others to help enrich their lives.

Nā Lālā

We run the Magic Hula Studio together, passing on the beautiful legacy of our mother. We impart our Christian upbringing to our students by beginning each session and performance with a prayer. We hold dear the many dances our mother choreographed and pay tribute to her through *mele* and dances that reflect the fragrant rose blossom. They tell of the irresistible essence of the flower and the regal beauty for which our mother was known and loved.

Akeakamai

We hope the passion and love for hula that our mother instilled in us will be embraced and cherished by generations that follow. Rose Joshua will be seen through our hands and remain in our hearts for all eternity.

Mana'o Pūlama

We have many wonderful memories of taking the enchantment of Hawai'i to different countries, sharing the warmth and beauty of the aloha spirit. Some of these include participating in Green Week in Berlin, Germany; opening the Mikazuki Hotel in Katsaura Chiba, Japan; flying with the Hawaiian Airlines promotions team; coordinating shows for the T. H. Davis Cruise Lines; and performing at the Mauna Loa Nightclub in Mexico City.

Ho'okō 'Ana

Our passion for hula enabled us to travel the world over as teachers and professional dancers. Blossom utilized her special talent as choreographer, creating unforgettable routines and unique shows. In 1963 we went on a military tour of Germany, Italy, Spain, France, and other European countries.

Rose Joshua

Magic Hula Studio

Nā Hoaloha O Ka Roselani No'eau

O'ahu

Kumu Hula
Wade Kilohana Shirkey

Nā Lālā

I recently spoke to a local *hālau* about my late *kumu*, Auntie Rose Joshua. As we discussed the underlying *kaona*—identifying steps, Auntie Rose's style, and recurring themes—I noticed that the students were using my experience to translate Hawaiian culture in general. Ever mindful that I owe my place in the culture to the blessings of Auntie Rose, Betty Hi'ilaniwai Atkinson, and Enoka Kaina, I remembered that I would always be a guest in this wonderful tradition.

A woman in the *hālau* wagged an angry finger in my face. She stressed that I had been embraced by several master teachers and that it was now time for me to give back. I sought counsel from Lorraine Daniel, Auntie Rose's daughter and *kumu* of Magic Hula Studio, which I called home for the past forty years. Soon after, our *hālau* was born.

I always say that God put the necessary elements of life into my footsteps: hula, Hawaiian language, and writing about the most beautiful culture in the most beautiful place on earth. But it was actually Auntie Betty, my *hānai* mom, who nudged me onto that path.

Akeakamai

Long ago I decided that I would pass on the knowledge from my hula mentors by including not only the songs and music Auntie Rose imparted to me, but also the spirit, sense of family, and joy of sitting at a master's feet and learning. If Auntie Rose hadn't made hula both meaningful and enjoyable, I wouldn't have continued for what has become a lifetime. Consequently, we try in our *hālau* to make the experience as much fun as it is educational.

Some of our students have been with us for more than ten years. Sons and daughters are now joining their mothers in class. Our *hālau* has included elementary school students, senior citizens, Catholic nuns, military wives, and everyone in between.

Mana'o Pūlama

Our motto is "We can never fill her shoes. We can but walk in her footsteps." Our *hālau* name reflects this motto—Nā Hoaloha O Ka Roselani No'eau means "The Beloved Companions of the Wise Rose." We express our love for Auntie Rose and perpetuate her teachings and wisdom as a group of friends.

Ho'okō 'Ana

It is now quite common for former students to meet in a crowd and exclaim, "I know you! You used to dance for Kilohana!"

Nā Hoaloha O Ka Roselani Noʻeau

Aloha,
Brian + Dan
love,
[signature]

Nā Hula 'O Kaleiokapualani

Based on O'ahu, we have been sharing the faith, hope, and love of God with *nā haumāna, nā 'ohana,* and all people since 1995.

Kumu Hula
Hi'ilei Silva

Nā Lālā
Though based on the names of my two daughters (Kaleiokalani and Kapualani), who assist me with the *hālau, kaleiokapualani* literally means "the garland of the heavenly flower."

The *kaona* is "the beloved child of the heavenly flower." For us, the beloved child is every child in the *hālau;* the heavenly flower is Jesus.

Our *hālau* is grateful to have touched so many people's lives in the islands, the continental U.S, and the Philippines. At all of our performances, we believe that God is revealed through the beauty and grace of hula.

Akeakamai
The *hālau* motto is *"E halelū lākou i Kona inoa me ka ha'a āna.* Let them praise His name with dancing. Psalm 149:3 NIV."

Mana'o Pūlama
During a mission to the Philippines in Olangapo City, we sang and danced hula for an audience of seventy street children, who come into the facility each week to eat, receive medical attention, and play together. As we performed, the children's faces lit up with joy and wonder. Most of them had never seen hula or anything Hawaiian in person. They enjoyed our performance so much that we gave them a short lesson on a few basic steps.

Ho'okō 'Ana
We recently participated in the Queen Lili'uokalani *Keiki* Hula Competition. We did not go there to compete, but to share our mission with the hope that we would touch many hearts.

Nā Hula 'O Kaleiokapualani

Naipo Nā Mea Hula

Based on Oʻahu, we have entertained Hawaiʻi and beyond for the past fifteen years.

Kumu Hula

Leinaʻala Naipo Akamine led a *hālau* of both men and women coworkers at Verizon Hawaiʻi before offering her first hula class at Kamehameha Schools in 1989. She has also taught *hula ʻauana* at the YWCA and the Kapahulu Senior Center.

Kūʻauhau

My parents, siblings, and ancestors come from Kapaʻau, a tiny district in North Kohala. Whenever I visit this *ʻāina*, I can feel the divine powers of all my *kūpuna*.

Nā Lālā

Our members include businesspeople, homemakers, and high school and university students. Every summer, we try to attend the weekend Papa Kanaka O Puʻu Koholā *Heiau* workshops in Kawaihae. These workshops include sunrise ceremonies, visits to sacred temples, presentations by guest speakers, a delicious traditional feast, and several hula performances. The weekend ends with church services at Pelekane and a craft fair where participants can learn traditional Hawaiian arts.

Akeakamai

I believe in perpetuating hula and *oli* so future generations can understand and appreciate our ancestors' cultural and traditional values. I feel a tremendous need to share as much as possible with all who are willing to learn.

Manaʻo Pūlama

Our *hālau* has been privileged to participate in many cultural ceremonies—chanting for the Hawaiʻi Drug Court Program and Queen Liliʻuokalani's Centennial Observance, dancing on the rim of Halemaʻumaʻu Crater in honor of Pele, and accompanying the sacred sash of Līloa in a solemn procession from Maunaʻala to ʻIolani Palace. We also took part in the *hoʻokupu* and performances at the Ua Ao Hawaiʻi concerts and did the *oli* at Maunaʻala to memorialize the signing of Ke Aliʻi Bernice Pauahi Bishop's last will and testament. In addition, our *hula kahiko* presentation for the Myriam Halberstam Film Production was recently broadcast throughout Europe.

Hoʻokō ʻAna

In 1999 we traveled to Rapa Nui, also known as Easter Island, to celebrate the *Hōkūleʻa*'s completion of its Polynesian Triangle Voyage.

Performing and chanting before the Moai, planting koa seedlings to reforest the island, helping to build a circular stone temple, and visiting sacred sites were among the highlights of our trip.

Since 1992 we have participated in the King Kamehameha Celebration Floral Parade Commercial Decorated Vehicles Division, winning numerous first-place awards and other commendations. A photo of an award-winning entry and our *hālau* performing is on display at the Smithsonian Institution.

Naipo Nā Mea Hula

Nā Malama Polynesian Dance Studio

'Ewa Beach, O'ahu

Kumu Hula

Kau'ionalani Serrao believes that learning is a never-ending process. Only through knowledge has she been able to take part in preserving the beauty of the Hawaiian culture. She currently studies with Kumu Kimo Alama Keaulana at Lei Hulu Hula School, where she joined the *hula 'ōlapa* class in 1998.

Kū'auhau

In the mid '60s, I began my life of hula at the 'Ewa Beach Parks and Recreation with Kumu Hula Lou Valdez. She was a great influence in my love for hula and taught me how to play the ukulele. I also learned from Ku'ulei Clark, who introduced me to a variety of Polynesian dances.

In addition to later dancing with Nā Kumu Dennise Kia and Denise Ramento of the Aloha Pumehana Polynesian Dance Studio (formerly known as Pupukahi Otea), I danced for Kealoha Kalama at the Bishop Museum and represented the Hawai'i Visitors Bureau with her in Japan and London.

My greatest mentor is Vicky Holt Takamine, whose Pua Ali'i 'Ilima group marked the beginning of my *hula kahiko* training. In 1981, we entered our first Merrie Monarch Festival competition. It was also Vicky who encouraged me in 1993 to start teaching.

Nā Lālā

In 1993, I established Nā Malama Polynesian Dance Studio as a non-competitive *hālau* solely to perpetuate and maintain tradition so our younger generation could enjoy what our *kūpuna* left behind.

I teach my *haumāna* that hula is not about competition, but about sharing, loving, and preserving the art. My belief in traditional hula has taught them to respect and value the Hawaiian culture and its people.

Akeakamai

When we're together, we understand that our bonds and feelings of togetherness as an *'ohana* are what this *hālau* is all about.

Ho'okō 'Ana

My life has been busy, but filled with hula, my first love. I feel blessed to have performed at so many wonderful venues throughout Hawai'i, such as Germaine's Luau, Sea Life Park, Sky View Terrace, Hale Koa Hotel, Paradise Cove Luau, the Vic Leon Show in Waikīkī, and the Norm Sua Show at the Hyatt Regency Hotel. I have also been a solo dancer at the Outrigger Reef Hotel and danced at Chateau Akanazaki in Atami, Japan.

Nā Malama Polynesian Dance Studio

Na ʻOhana O Ke Ānuenue

Oʻahu

Kumu Hula

Taunja Paishon is the granddaughter of Pua Almeida and great-granddaughter of Johnny Almeida. Her Hawaiian bloodline and true aloha spirit shine through in her teaching.

Nā Lālā

Na ʻOhana O Ke Ānuenue is a product of young and old and of many different races. This is common of most *hālau*, with *kumu* embracing everyone with the same love and respect. Our *hālau* is unique because we all respect our *kumu* and each other with no feeling of competition or wanting to be better than someone else. When we get together, we have so much to share that our first half hour is usually spent just "talking story."

Auntie Taunja has always given so much to her students and our community. She offers our *hālau* to community functions without charging a fee, giving from the heart and never expecting anything in return.

Take the lehua *blossoms, red in beauty,*
Gather the ʻilima *petals, bright, orange, and so delicate,*
Give me strands and strands of the purest white pīkake,
Pick the tiny pakalana *blossoms with its morning-fresh fragrance,*
And the pua kenikeni *that turns three different colors before it matures,*
All of the beauty from each of the flowers intertwined,
Held fast by the strength of the vines of the maile.

This is our hālau, this is our kumu!
The beauty she brings, the delicate motions of the hula she creates,
The purest of love she has for her hula and for her students,
The "nahenahe" sweet and gentle voice she carries,
The stages that her students, young and old, go through before they truly understand why
HULA IS WHAT IT IS AND WHY WE LOVE TO DANCE!
Na ʻOhana O Ke Ānuenue is not only the Family of the Rainbow,
it is the true love that this hālau has, because of the strength and support we give to each other!

Manaʻo Pūlama

We have performed at countless events as varied as Aloha Week at the Aloha Tower, community functions, fundraisers, weddings, birthdays, and shopping malls.

Na ‘Ohana O Ke Ānuenue

Nā ʻŌpio O Koʻolau

Kāneʻohe

Kumu Hula

Although Michael and James Dela Cruz were never allowed formal hula lessons as children, they always knew what they were meant to do.

Kūʻauhau

Our first *kumu* was our mother, Louisa Kaleikula, who always encouraged us to sing at parties and at church. Our grandmother taught us to be seen and not heard. We had to learn with our eyes, ears, and senses just by being in the presence of the source.

Our first informal hula lessons began when **Nā Kumu Hula Luka** and Louise Kaleiki and their Ilima Hula Studio regularly performed at our church. We hid and *mahaʻoi* behind the curtains as the *hālau* rehearsed.

Our "real" *kumu* is Aloha Dalire. In the mid-1970s, we joined her Polynesian Happening *hālau* and sang with them at King's Alley in Waikīkī. From the side of the stage, we watched her teach and listened as she sang. When we got home, we taught each other what we saw, remembered, and absorbed.

Auntie Mattie Aberilla, ʻIhilani Miller, Sadette Sakawe, Ron Bright, Kalani Poʻomahealani, Uncle George Naʻope, Keala Kukona, Kawaikapu Hewett, Manu Boyd, and others have also inspired us.

Nā Lālā

In 1977, we formed a performing group that later became our *hālau*. Since then, we have taught our *haumāna* to use their bodies to make a difference in the lives of those who watch our performances. If we bring a tear to the audience's eyes or a smile to their faces, we know we are giving comfort to their hearts.

If you believe from deep within your *naʻau* that you are doing what you are supposed to do, things will always be *pono*. We teach this to our *haumāna*, while also instilling that they must feel the spirit of the dance from within. They must know what every word and costume means, as well as why every movement was created.

Akeakamai

If you believe in yourself, you can accomplish anything you want in life.

Manaʻo Pūlama

In 1981, we performed with Don Ho. It was so wonderful to work with this legend. After getting to know him, we understood why he is admired by so many.

Hoʻokō ʻAna

We were recently invited to be the closing act on *Good Morning America* in New York City. While our *hālau* danced, we prayed that the spirit of aloha in our songs would bring healing to the people of New York.

Nā Pualei O Kauno‘a

Lāna‘i

Kumu Hula
Born and raised on Maui, Rita Moon spent a few years living on the mainland before the islands called her back home in 1975.

Kū‘auhau
I started dancing *hula ‘auana* with Doll Aricayos in Lahaina, Maui. In November 1978, I moved to Lana‘i and met Elaine La‘ikealohaihalona Ka‘opuiki, who became my *kumu* for the next fifteen years. Though her forte was *hula ‘auana*, she still gave me a good foundation in *hula kahiko*.

Nā Lālā
In March 1992, I was given a traditional *‘ūniki* and with my *kumu*’s blessing, I opened Na Pualei O Kauno‘a. For three years we entered the Ka‘anapali Beach Hotel Keiki Hula Competition, but have since become a non-competing *hālau*.

Most of my *haumāna* are Filipina and are exposed to the Hawaiian culture and history through hula and in school. I try to give them a real sense of what it’s like to grow up in a Hawaiian home, to be surrounded by and share so much aloha. This emphasis on culture also extends to our dancing. I teach my *haumāna* the steps and motions of the hula, as well as the history and meaning behind the *mele*.

Akeakamai
Our *hālau* is an extension of our homes. We share with and care for each other, making sure not to cause hurt by worry or deed. My *haumāna* become hula sisters, part of the *‘ohana*, not just acquaintances in dance. They learn to see and appreciate the beauty in one another and to nourish and nurture that special bond of aloha.

Mana‘o Pūlama
Living, teaching, and dancing on the small island of Lana‘i has been a beautiful and most rewarding experience for me and my *haumāna*. In our presentations and performances, we incorporate both *hula ‘auana* and *hula kahiko*.

Ho‘okō ‘Ana
Through hula my *haumāna* gain confidence, raise their self-esteem, and feel a greater sense of belonging. When they walk away from the *hālau* with even a small part of that, I am fulfilled.

Nā Pualei O Kauno‘a

U.S. Mainland

Aloha Polynesia!

Based in Sacramento, we have entertained Northern California for over twenty-five years.

Ke Po'o
Cheryl Cook is our director and events coordinator. Tyra Simoni is our dance teacher. Albert Fakalata, former manager of the famous Zombie Hut restaurant in Sacramento, has been our lead musician for over twenty years.

Kū'auhau
We have been honored to work with the late *kumu hula* Uncle John Manuia, who shared with us his rich knowledge of ancient Hawaiian culture.

Nā Lālā
We have *keiki* performers as young as three years old, dancers who have been *'ohana* members for over twenty-three years, and entire families who love to share the Polynesian culture and the spirit of aloha. We are Hawaiian, Samoan, Tongan, Filipino, Mexican, Chinese, Caucasian, Japanese, Native American, African American, Persian, and Micronesian. While we come from different ethnic backgrounds, we share a common bond, the love of Polynesian dance and culture. This is what makes us so special to each other, and this is what binds our *'ohana* together.

Akeakamai
We perform to celebrate the spirit and the dances of the Polynesian people. Each year, our Aloha *'ohana* sets exciting new goals, and we embark on new adventures all year long.

Mana'o Pūlama
We have performed at hundreds of community events and cultural fairs and at sporting events that include Sacramento Kings, San Francisco 49ers, and Stanford University halftime shows. We also regularly perform at luaus and at cultural assemblies at local schools. In 2003 we sent soloists to the Tahiti Fetes in Las Vegas and San Jose.

Ho'okō 'Ana
In 2002, our *'ohana* doubled in size, and in 2003 we nearly doubled in size again.

Aloha Polynesia!

The HULA Connection

Dana Point, California

Ke Poʻo

Linane Nahina Pfister feels fortunate to have been part of the enlightening Hawaiian Renaissance and privileged to have learned hula at a very young age. When she was a teenager, she was proud to be local—born with an enthusiasm for hula. She always felt an excitement and stirring within when watching or learning *hula kahiko* and traditional hula dances. Hula was a part of her no matter where she went. When she attended Pacific University in Oregon, she kept her cultural roots alive by helping other island students organize a Hawaiian club, teach and learn Polynesian dances, and plan annual luaus.

Kūʻauhau

Uncle Keola Beamer lived across the street from my family. He instilled in me the passion and respect for *oli*, which added to my experience of music and dance. I lived and breathed the aloha spirit.

At the University of Hawaiʻi, I minored in dance, studying *hula kahiko* with esteemed university *kumu* such as Uncle George Naʻope. In 1980 I became an active member in three halaus in California and danced professionally for Aunty Ilima and Uncle Jr. Montgomery for the following eighteen years.

Nā Lālā

After many years of dancing and training, I knew it was time to give back and share the knowledge of dance, traditions, and values of my upbringing by establishing The HULA Connection. Our *hālau* is actively involved with the Dana Point Youth and Group Facility, the Ocean Institute, and the Ocean Educational Center. Through educational, community, and public performances, we teach and perpetuate hula and the Hawaiian culture.

We teach our *haumāna* not only to dance, but also to learn the language, traditions, and most important, the values that are so intertwined with the culture. We encourage our *haumāna* to practice the aloha spirit with all those around them to bring a little more peace and love to the world.

My oldest son has been an inspiration to our *hālau keiki*. He enthusiastically shares his heritage with them by playing instruments, performing Hawaiian chants and dances, and retelling familiar legends in Pidgin English.

Akeakamai

Once you gain knowledge, it's important to give back and share it to perpetuate and keep our culture alive.

Manaʻo Pūlama

It deeply touches our souls when audiences at convalescent homes and other public venues shed tears at our performances.

*T*he *HULA* Connection

Motu Nehenehe Polynesian Dancers

Based in San Diego, we have been performing Tahitian, Hawaiian, Samoan, and New Zealand dances throughout southern California and parts of Nevada since 1990.

Ke Poʻo

Babe "Uʻilani" Valero credits hula as her introduction to the world of Polynesian dance, which led to her present career as a professional dancer, choreographer, costume designer, instructor, model, and Hawaiian retail shop owner. She has modeled for well-known Hawaiian art photographer Randy Jay Braun. A life-size bronze statue on the front grounds of the Hilton Hawaiian Village Hotel in Waikīkī was based on one of his photos of her.

Kūʻauhau

I danced for a few months on the island of Bora Bora, French Polynesia, under the famous Tahitian dance director Coco Ella Cote.

Nā Lālā

Motu nehenehe means "beautiful island" in Tahitian; it signifies all the beautiful aspects of island life—the sights, sounds, songs, dances, and especially the people. Our group consists of approximately eighty *haumāna*, all varying in age and ethnic background. When you join the group, you are not just a member, but a part of the Motu ʻohana. It's an extended family where lifelong friendships are developed and much love and aloha are shared. We believe and understand that hula is a privilege. The success of our group is attributed to the love of God and one another, a belief in sharing, and mutual respect for all.

Akeakamai

Hula is a self-transforming experience that only another hula dancer can understand. You feel such a harmonious feeling when dancing hula; it engulfs your whole being. A good hula dancer not only knows her dance, but also feels it from within. It's a mind-soul connection when your steps are coordinated with the music, your hands, your head, and your heart. Once you become hooked on hula, there is no turning back. It becomes an important part of your life, both inside and outside the hula studio.

Hula lifts your spirits. It's also an experience you share with audiences as they, too, respond with enjoyment and appreciation of your dance.

Hoʻokō ʻAna

Many parents tell me how hula has transformed their shy children into self-confident, assertive people. Children who dance hula are more active in social activities and become good students, good performers, good team players, and basically just good kids all around.

Motu Nehenehe Polynesian Dancers

Hālau Hula ʻO Nā Mauna Komohana

Founded in 1993 in Boulder, Colorado

Ke Poʻo

Miriam Pumehana Paisner

Kūʻauhau

I had the opportunity to study hula under the tutelage of Hoʻoulu Cambra, Hoakalei Kamauʻu, Nona Beamer, Rose Joshua, Kawaikapuokalani Hewett, and Kealoha Kalama. Each of these great *kumu* gave me unforgettable knowledge of the beauty of the hula. It is with great respect to each of my mentors that I now pass on this knowledge, upholding the traditions, authenticity, and cherished aloha.

Nā Lālā

Our group is the first in Colorado to have live chanting and *mele* for our *kahiko* and *ʻauana*. Unlike many, and out of deep respect, I do not call myself Kumu nor do my *haumāna ʻūniki*. We are a *hālau* in the Western sense of the word. Unable to gather flowers and plants to make lei and other adornments, my *haumāna* are taught to make and design their own *pāʻū, muʻumuʻu,* and silk lei. We memorize our *oli* and embrace *hula kahiko* and traditional *mele ʻauana,* rarely dancing to *hapa haole* numbers. In our performances, we try to teach the audiences about the beauty and some of the history of ancient and modern Hawaiʻi.

Akeakamai

I am a firm believer in cultural and political sovereignty and try to pass on this *aloha ʻāina*—love for the land and all that is on it—to my *haumāna*. I feel strongly that just teaching dancers to hula without teaching them the cultural, sociopolitical, and environmental history of Hawaiʻi is a waste of time. If one wants to learn hula, I believe one should also learn about the unique culture that encompasses Hawaiʻi, including its beautiful language. My students also learn that Hawaiʻi was upheld by a people who believed in their own gods and goddesses. Even if one does not believe in them, one must respect this belief.

Manaʻo Pūlama

My greatest dream was to present the community with a performance and reading of *Liliʻuokalani*, a play written by the late Aldyth Morris of Hawaiʻi. With the blessings of her son, my dream came true last summer. We interspersed chant, hula, and *mele* where they best fit historically and culturally. We dedicated it to the *kanaka maoli*, the native Hawaiian people, and their struggle to raise their beloved nation, Lāhui Aloha, once more. *ʻOnipaʻa.*

Hālau Hula 'O Nā Mauna Komohana

Hālau Punani ‘Ohelohelo

Formed in 1986 in Littleton, Colorado

Ke Po‘o
Alyce Polak Blevins

Kū‘auhau

I owe my philosophy and unwavering attention to ancient methods to Palani Kahala, a highly respected *kumu hula*. Following his death, I continued studying under Mapuana DeSilva and Vicky Takamine. I was blessed with three wonderful mentors who allowed me to be me.

Nā Lālā

We are a traditional *hālau* focusing on hula only, both *kahiko* and modern-style *‘auana*. We have 120 dedicated students from all corners of the nation and the world, of all different ethnicities and cultures. My first students were my daughter Carol and her best friend. Carol passed away at the age of twenty-six. She was by my side through all the growth and growing pains of starting up the *hālau*. She was always my supporter and my behind-the-scenes shoulder. She is still the whisper in my ear, the smile on my face, and the hug for all my dancers.

Sometimes talent and community come together in the most unexpected places. In land-locked Colorado, where instead of palm trees and tropical breezes, mountains and plains are the unlikely backdrop, I have *‘ohana* as *kumu* of Puanani‘ohelohelo. In true Hawaiian style, the *keiki* of this *hālau* are *hānai*, relatives not by blood but by heart. This sentiment runs deep throughout Puanani‘ohelohelo.

Everyone is an auntie or a cousin, and it is not uncommon to see multiple generations from one family within the *hālau*. Grandmothers in their sixties can be found dancing alongside grandchildren as young as three.

Akeakamai

Hula is an art form as well as a unifying force. Even having taught hula for nearly twenty years now, I still return to the touchstone of what hula represents to me. Inspired by ancient traditions, rhythm, music, movement, and grace, hula ignites a common passion among people of all cultures. Hula teaches me to respect all cultures and the traditions of the past. Staying connected to the Hawaiian culture while residing in Colorado is a common theme for the families of Puanani‘ohelohelo. King Kalākaua perhaps said it best, *"Hula is the language of the heart, therefore the heartbeat of the Hawaiian people."*

Hālau Punani 'Ohelohelo

Hālau Hula Kaleooka'iwa

Orlando, Florida

Kumu Hula

Kawehi Punahele says that his need to perpetuate the Hawaiian culture has always preceded his professional and personal goals.

Kū'auhau

I consider myself blessed by Ke Akua and all of my *kūpuna kahiko*. I am lucky to be part of a treasured and talented musical family; my grandfather played music with the Kalama Boys. Though I have also been fortunate to be mentored by many *kumu* and *kumu hula* through the decades, I will forever cherish the wisdom and stories of Kumu Hula Robert Cazimero.

Nā Lālā

I often challenge my *haumāna* to walk away from our *hālau* with "time capsules" and strong memories of the aloha we spent together. I try to keep the chants and hulas taught to me as pure as possible, as they serve as direct links to our past. I constantly create new *kahiko* and *'auana* hulas to memorialize the present, my life at this time. I look to my *haumāna*, the *'ōpiopio*, the future of our culture, and try to nurture them the way my mentors nurtured me.

Before my *haumāna* can dance with expression and feeling, they must understand the story behind the *mele* or *oli*. I assign them to research these meanings by contacting composers such as Keali'i Reichel, Mark Keali'i Ho'omalu, and Manu Boyd. When the *kumu hula* share the thoughts behind their *mele*, they truly exemplify the aloha spirit and teach my *haumāna* about the importance of staying true to the *mele* in their performances. A crucial part of hula is incorporating the body, mind, and spirit. When the physical movements are in unison with an understanding of what the moves mean, the beauty of the story or *mana'o* behind the story shines through.

Akeakamai

We remember our past through an adherence to tradition. We remember our present by continuing to create new chants and hulas for the future. Sometimes simply singing a song or chanting an *oli* can realign our spirits and point us in the right direction.

Mana'o Pūlama

After my *hālau* shared the hula "Nani Hanalei," a *tūtū* (grandmother) born and raised on the mainland thanked me for taking her home. I smiled, thanked her, and asked when she last visited her island home. "Never," she said, "but I could feel all the places you danced about and I was there."

Hālau Hula Kaleooka'iwa

Nā 'Ōpiopio I Orlando

Orlando, Florida

Kumu Hula

In the 1960s, Kau'i Healani Brandt taught Tahitian at Waikīkī's International Market Place and coordinated the annual Tahiti Fete competitions, bringing in people from all over the world.

Kū'auhau

When I was eight years old, I began studying hula with Pansy Stagner. She enriched my life and gave me a great foundation. Since then, I have had the opportunity to study under hula greats such as Ku'ulei Clarke, Rose Joshua, Loke Nuhi, Bella Richards, and Uncle George Na'ope. They all played such an important role in shaping who I am today.

Nā Lālā

In the 1970s, I coordinated and emceed Kau'i's Pono Polynesian Revue at the Polynesian Resort in Disney World. Beginning with a cast of seven, we grew to a cast of thirty-five by 1979. I have since been working as a cultural representative at the Polynesian Resort Hotel. Our guests come from all over the world. We greet them with leis of aloha and teach them basic hula steps and motions as well as the intricate art of lei-making. Being greeted with a lei and a hug is many visitors' first experience of the Hawaiian tradition of aloha.

On Saturdays I teach hula classes at the hotel and encourage local *keiki* and hotel guests to participate. These classes are conducted *manuahi,* free of charge. Kahikili Brandon and Kawehi Punahele often join me, offering their time so generously to perpetuate the beauty of the hula.

Many *kumu hula,* such as Chinky Māhoe, Keali'i Reichel, and members of the Kanaka'ole family, come from Hawai'i to conduct hula seminars each year. These seminars allow us to experience different styles of dancing, gather further knowledge, and spend time with people from home.

Akeakamai

Hula must live on through our children.

Ho'okō 'Ana

Since 1978, I've traveled each year to Michigan to conduct private classes for teachers only. They come to me from various states and are so eager to learn. I instill the importance of dancing correctly, learning the history of Hawai'i, and understanding the *mana'o* of the *mele* and the dance. If they are to carry on the culture, it must be *pono.*

The Barefoot Hawaiian

Based in Illinois, we have been performing for the past twenty years.

Kumu Hula

Gwen Adair Keake'akamai Kennedy has been dancing since she was three years old, when her mother enrolled her in the first Hawaiian dance class offered in their area. Gwen continued her training while growing up, celebrating her 'ūniki in Chicago before teaching hula out of her home in high school and eventually opening a Hawaiian shop, office, and hula studio with her mother.

Kū'auhau

In the 1950s, many Hawaiians and others of Polynesian descent moved to Chicago to start new lives. Most were entertainers from Hawai'i. I was fortunate to be trained by those pioneers who left their tropical climates to come to the land of wind and snow! They found work at Chicago's only Hawaiian restaurant at the time, Honolulu Harry's Club Waikiki, where my sister and I soon performed with other keiki and adults.

Many years ago, my mother did everything possible to give my sister and me the opportunity to experience hula, part of a very unique culture that existed so far away from us. She had seen Hawai'i only in pictures and movies but fell in love with the islands and what they stood for—paradise. Today, what was once only a dream for my mother is now a reality in our daily lives. Hula was her gift to me. She did not teach me, but she opened the door and encouraged me to step inside. And now her gift is my way of life.

Nā Lālā

Blessed by a Hawaiian priest in 1983,

our hālau has more than one hundred members—kāne, wāhine, and keiki—of all ages.

Akeakamai

I believe that we are not individual "owners" of places, things, or ideas in this life, but ambassadors for God's endless work. We are each given blessings to carry out divine ideas; in doing so we contribute to the ever-changing plan of the universe.

Mana'o Pūlama

We regularly perform in more than five hundred shows throughout the country each year. The most valuable performances to me are those for the less fortunate in hospitals and senior homes. Most of those people will never travel to Hawai'i, so I am proud to have the opportunity to share the islands with them.

Ho'okō 'Ana

In 2003, our twentieth year, we were invited to perform internationally in Shanghai, China.

Hālau Pūlama Mau Ke Aloha Ka ʻOhana ʻIlima

Based in Pasadena, Maryland, we have been performing since October 1990.

Kumu Hula

Kas Keolapua Nakamura's heart was touched by hula when she first visited Hawaiʻi in 1972. Kas soon joined ʻIlima Hula Studio, which won first place at the 1975 Merrie Monarch Festival. ʻIlima was one of only three *hālau* doing *hula kahiko* at the competition.

Kūʻauhau

We are richly nourished by the foundational values of the late Nā Kumu Hula Luka and Louise Kaleiki, ʻIlima Hula Studio, Honolulu.

Nā Lālā

We participated in the Bishop Museum's 2003 exhibit on hula around the world. We sponsor hula and craft workshops by visiting *kumu hula* and *kūpuna* from Hawaiʻi, publish our *hālau* email newsletter DRUMBEATS, present cultural exhibits and luaus, and enter competitions. With each competition, we gain insight and friendship.

Hālau hula is indeed a sharing of life, particularly with our sister *hālau* Ka Leo O Ka ʻIwa, Kumu Hula Kawehi Punahele (Florida), and our rootlet, Hālau Pūlama Mau Ke Aloha Ka ʻOhana ʻIlima O Kololako, Kumu and Alakaʻi ʻOhana Gutierrez (Colorado).

Akeakamai

Our hula style and *manaʻo* reflect those of ʻIlima and the Kaleiki sisters—our *hālau*'s name means the "Hula School to Cherish Always with Love the Family ʻIlima." We look at our *hālau* wall to see the 1975 newspaper article on the Merrie Monarch Festival and know that success is possible with hard work and a grounded foundation.

Manaʻo Pūlama

We've participated in the following events: World Hula Invitational, Oʻahu, 1992; Ke Ānuenue, Washington state, 1993; Hula O Nā Keiki, Maui, 1993, 1995; Ka Hula Leʻa, Hawaiʻi, 1996, 2000; Hōʻike Hawaiʻi, Florida, 1999.

Hoʻokō ʻAna

At the 1997 Ka Hula Leʻa competition in Hawaiʻi, we won third place in the Kupuna Division. At the same competition in 2000, we won the Judges' Trophy and placed third in the Keiki Kāne Division.

Hālau Pūlama Mau Ke Aloha Ka ʻOhana ʻIlima

Ānuenue Dance Company

Dearborn, Michigan

Ke Poʻo
Janeen Bodary

Kūʻauhau
Janeen first become interested in hula when her father, knowing how she loved to dance, brought a beautiful pair of ʻuliʻulī home with him from a business trip. Sarah Paull, with whom Janeen studied hula from the age of six, was a continuous source of inspiration for her.

Nā Lālā
When it was first founded in September 2001, the dance company had only five haumāna. Although spiritually diverse, the dancers are dedicated to proving that the true aloha spirit reaches far beyond the borders of the Hawaiian Islands.

Akeakamai
Janeen's goal is to preserve and pass on the practices of hula. She also shares the aloha that Mrs. Paull shared with her. The "Circle," a tradition handed down from Mrs. Paull, is practiced before each performance. Through the simple act of joining hands, the dancers wordlessly connect to each other and receive the necessary energy to perform. Janeen sees this tradition as a necessary transition from rehearsal to performance because it provides a physical and emotional connection between her and her haumāna as well as a valuable spiritual connection to Mrs. Paull and to her God.

Manaʻo Pūlama
Ānuenue performs hula kahiko in honor of King Kalākaua and Queen Liliʻuokalani; the hālau's first-time visit to ʻIolani Palace in July 2002 was therefore humbling and inspiring. Visiting Hawaiʻi and its historical sites greatly expanded the dancers' appreciation and understanding of hula. They are anticipating a return to the islands in July 2004 and hope to visit Kīlauea Volcano to gain a deeper appreciation for the dances they perform for Hiʻiaka and Pele.

Hoʻokō ʻAna
Firmly believing that all knowledge is not contained within one body or place, Janeen attends workshops and seminars on hula. She also researches the people, places, language, and stories of Hawaiʻi with different nā kumu hula whenever the opportunity arises. She encourages her haumāna to do the same.

Ānuenue Dance Company

Hālau Hoʻoleʻaleʻa (Aloha Paradise Dancers)

Detroit, Michigan

Ke Poʻo

Judith Mikiʻala Williams-Huddleston

Kūʻauhau

I have many people to thank for keeping me on the path of sharing my knowledge of hula and for pushing me forward: Mapuana—my friend and inspiration—now living her dream on Oʻahu; ʻUala in Utah who is never far from my *puʻuwai*; Keola and Nā Kumu Keoni and Kalaʻi at the University of Hawaiʻi-Hilo (what a job they have had!); and the many *kumu hula* I've been fortunate to study under; also, my hula sister Dahmia for her truly unconditional friendship.

Nā Lālā

Our *hālau* is an *ʻohana* that stems from many communities.

Akeakamai

In my teachings of this magnificent dance, I try to impart the importance of *ʻohana*. It is my sincerest hope that others will continue to guide us, to show us, and to make our *manaʻo pono* so that when our hula comes to us from the heart and mind, it will always reflect the beauty, grace, and culture of Hawaiʻi.

As we have been given the beauty of the hula, we feel it is also important to give back. It is because of this importance that we, as a hula *ʻohana*, participate in the annual Thanksgiving Festival of Trees, a benefit for the local children's hospital. It fills our lives with so much joy as we gather together each year to create magnificent wreaths and gingerbread houses that are donated to this wonderful cause. This annual tradition is but a small way for us to say *mahalo* for the happiness hula brings to our lives.

Manaʻo Pūlama

After we first shared song and dance with Lukela Kalekiko, he wrote: "*Auē!* The women of the Hālau Hoʻoleʻaleʻa are just awesome! As a proud Hawaiian living far away from home, they made me feel as though part of my Hawaiian culture wasn't lost here in the Midwest. Mikiʻala, your knowledge of the language and the hula made me feel like I was home in the islands. These women truly have shown the *mana* of our culture."

Hālau Hoʻoleʻaleʻa (Aloha Paradise Dancers)

Pacific Island Dancers

Cedar Springs, Michigan

Ke Poʻo

Minnie Morey remembers cultural music and dance playing an important role in her everyday family life.

Kūʻauhau

As a young adult, I was introduced to Philippine folk dance teacher Bernardo Pedere, who became my lifelong teacher and friend. Bernardo organized the Filipina Dance Troupe in California, and continues to teach traditional folk dances to a group of Filipino dancers.

My love of hula began when I met Keaulani, a hula instructor who taught me the basic steps of hula. Several years later, I put together a cultural performance for a community festival in Michigan. The audience response was so positive that I contacted the Foundation for Pacific Dance in Colorado in search of a *kumu*. The Foundation informed me of a weeklong workshop in Honolulu that would bring together many of the top *kumu hula*.

The workshop opened my mind to the world of hula. There I met the late Kumu Hula Palani Kahala, Kumu Hula Chinky Māhoe, and other instructors who all accepted my invitation to be part of several hula workshops in Michigan.

Nā Lālā

While I continued my education, attending hula and Polynesian workshops in Hawaiʻi, Indiana, and California, my *hālau* grew with the addition of more friends, relatives, and co-workers. Today we perform cultural dances from Hawaiʻi, Tahiti, the Philippines, and New Zealand. People are often surprised when they learn that a group of dancers who study traditional hula and other island cultures exists in Michigan.

Akeakamai

My love and respect for the Hawaiian Islands is demonstrated through our performances. We not only entertain but also educate the audience about the history and culture of the Hawaiian people. What a beautiful culture the Hawaiian people have to share with the world, and the Pacific Island Dancers and I are so fortunate to be part of it!

Manaʻo Pūlama

Some members of the *hālau* traveled for the first time to Hawaiʻi in 2001 to perform for the passengers and crew of the historical *SS Independence* as it cruised around the major islands. The Hawaiian people who watched our performances were ecstatic about our aloha spirit.

Hoʻokō ʻAna

My most memorable accomplishment was being asked to help two Michigan women prepare for the 1989 Miss America and 1993 Ms. Senior America competitions. I offered music and choreography suggestions to Miss Michigan Kaye Lani Raftko and Ms. Senior Michigan Jonsie Sturgis, who both took home national titles.

Pacific Island Dancers

Polynesian Fantasy Dancers (Pi'ilani Wahines)

Based in Detroit, Michigan, the Polynesian Fantasy Dancers/Pi'ilani Wahines perform at about ninety events each year.

Ke Po'o

Frances Claire Price (Auntie Fran) began dancing hula in 1970 and has since become a "gypsy teacher," teaching hula five days a week at various locations throughout the metropolitan area of Detroit. With a strong desire to learn more about Polynesian dance and culture, she attends every hula seminar in Indianapolis, Indiana, and frequently questions new instruction, styles, and techniques to ensure their authenticity before sharing them with her students. Hula is as much a part of Auntie Fran's life as breathing, eating, and sleeping.

Kū'auhau

Auntie Fran's teachers have included prominent members of the Polynesian dance community: Kau'i Brandt, Bill Charmin, Charlene Shelford-Lum, Pulefano Galea'i, Chinky Mahoe, Karo Mariteragi, Olana Ai, Ellen Gay Delarosa, Cathy Teriipaia, Leina'ala Heine Kalama, Sonny Ching, Keali'i Reichel, and Moon Kauakahi of the Mākaha Sons. Her biggest inspiration is Keith Awai.

Nā Lālā

One of many perks students of Auntie Fran enjoy is the treasure trove of costumes, implements, jewelry, and accessories she has amassed over the years. Students also benefit from Auntie's profound love of hula, which radiates through her body and soul as she dances and teaches. Her enduring aloha spirit is like a warm hug from a loving aunt—so endearing to both students and audiences.

Akeakamai

Hula is about perseverance and never giving up, even when faced with obstacles that seem insurmountable. When Auntie Fran took her first hula lesson at the age of thirty-two, she often felt overwhelmed and frustrated by the complexities of the Hawaiian language and dance. But with dedication and practice, her talent soon blossomed. A decade later, she was putting hundreds of miles on her minivan, traveling throughout Detroit to share the joy of hula with others.

Mana'o Pūlama

The Polynesian Fantasy Dancers/Pi'ilani Wahines once performed for a crowd of 6,000 at "Senior Power Day" in Canada. They also regularly perform at churches, private homes, country clubs, and various charitable events.

Ho'okō 'Ana

Hula has helped Auntie Fran overcome many difficult times in her life. She drew on its therapeutic qualities to cope with the death of her eldest son and has sought guidance from the spiritual teachings of the Hawaiian culture to better understand and discern information about hula.

Polynesian Fantasy Dancers (Pi'ilani Wahines)

Hālau Kaleiokapilialoha

Roseville, Minnesota

Kumu Hula

Dana Marie Kaleina'ala 'O Ka'ahuiona'li'i Enstad has been dancing hula since she was ten years old. Soon after graduating from Kamehameha Schools, she moved to Minnesota and immersed herself in the world of hula, dancing for a few luaus and small Polynesian shows around town. She taught hula at several local community centers but discovered that an eight-week class was not fully satisfying her love of spreading the aloha spirit. This realization, along with the encouragement of a few hula teachers, helped Dana understand her destiny—to share hula with anyone who is willing to learn.

Kū'auhau

My first hula teacher was Kaleo Colburn, who taught at the Rosalie Dance Academy in 'Aiea, where I danced for six years. I was also in the hula club at Kamehameha Schools under the tutelage of Mapuana DeSilva. After graduation I danced for several years in Japan and the United States, and then made Minnesota my home away from home.

It was in Minnesota that I met my late friend Maka, another Hawaiian transplant, who was gracious enough to let me join his *hālau*. After his death in 1996, one of his *haumāna*, Leona 'Uala Schroeder, continued the *hālau* for a few years before passing it on to me. Without Maka and Leona, my *hālau* would not be what it is today.

Nā Lālā

Kaleiokapilialoha means "the lei of close friendships," which represents what our *hālau* is about. Each *haumāna* is a *pua*, each unique in ethnicity, interest, profession, and knowledge. Together we form a lei of friendship and togetherness.

Since 2001, our *hālau* has grown from an *'ohana* of eight to an *'ohana* of twenty! There are no interviews or auditions to join the *hālau*; all that is needed is the desire to learn. I am fortunate to have such great *haumāna*. I couldn't have hand-picked a better *hālau*.

Akeakamai

Performing is not the sole purpose of our *hālau*. We live in a place enveloped in winter weather, so we warm our hearts and souls with hula and the aloha of our *hālau 'ohana*. We make the time and commitment to come together to share our love of Hawai'i and its culture, expressing this through the beauty of hula.

Ho'okō 'Ana

We will be performing for our second year at the Festival of Nations, which is quite a big deal for all ethnic groups in Minnesota.

Hālau Kaleiokapilialoha

Hālau Ka Waikahe Lani Malie and Hālau Kahulaliwai

Flathead Valley in northwest Montana has witnessed the flourishing of hula since 1993.

Kōkua Kumu:
Oʻahu native Macy Tadena Massey, under her former McKinley High School classmate Blaine Kamalani Kia

Kūʻauhau
Blaine Kamalani Kia, a renowned *kumu hula* and Hawaiian entertainer and the founder of the Ka Lauaʻe Foundation.

Nā Lālā
We are a nonprofit organization with male and female students ranging in age from six to seventy-four. The students, from towns such as Whitefish, Somers, Columbia Falls, Kalispell (where some girls have danced hula since they were three years old), and Bigfork drive in snow conditions to learn hula, and wear sweatpants under their *pāʻū* skirts when the building's heater isn't working!

Akeakamai
Our *hālau* mission is to perpetuate hula traditions and oral history in a grassroots, direct manner by teaching the students to support and respect the hula art form as well as Hawaiian culture and people. Here in this valley near the famed Glacier National Park, with its colorful mountain flowers, crisp, snow-capped mountains, large bodies of water to paddle on, catch fish and swim in, and bright stars filling what seems to be an endless sky, the connection to the *ʻāina* is felt strongly, just as it is in Hawaiʻi. It is no wonder that Montana's largest hula *hālau* attracts not only the Hawaiʻi natives now living here, but Hawaiians at heart who have absolute aloha for the hula.

Hoʻokō ʻAna
Following *kumu hula* Blaine Kia's involvement in 2003, the school, originally called Paradise Productions, became The Ladies of Hālau Ka Waikahe Lani Malie and The Men of Hālau Kahulaliwai.

Hālau Ka Waikahe Lani Malie and Hālau Kahulaliwai

Hālau Hula ʻO Wikolia (Gallery Kauaʻi)

Pittsford, New York

Kumu Hula

Victoria Wikolia Visiko dreamed of becoming a hula dancer when she was just four years old and began taking hula lessons as a *keiki*. Throughout her career, she has performed both in Hawaiʻi and on the mainland, winning the acceptance and gaining the love of many local Hawaiian musicians. She dedicates her life to spreading aloha to others through music, art, and hula, her life's passion.

Kūʻauhau

I have studied hula throughout the years with various *kumu*, but in February 2004 I began a new journey with Kumu Mapuana de Silva from Hālau Mohala ʻIlima on Oʻahu.

Nā Lālā

Many years ago, while I was performing in the islands, a *kumu hula* I didn't know told me to go back to the mainland and start a *hālau*. Hālau Hula ʻO Wikolia, affectionately called Gallery Kauaʻi, opened in 2001 and currently has a steady population of nearly fifty *haumāna*. We strive to become a Hawaiian culture and performance center.

My students respect the knowledge and love I have for the Hawaiian culture. They learn about the culture through the different styles of hula, both *ʻauana* and *kahiko*, and chant. They have also learned that it is *pono* to spread the aloha spirit, not only through hula, but through living it in small and large ways every day.

I also teach hula at various schools during the year to thousands of students of all ages. In addition to hula, I will begin teaching classes in Hawaiian studies and other styles of Polynesian dance.

Akeakamai

The *hālau*'s main purpose is to perpetuate the Hawaiian culture and spread the aloha spirit in upstate New York and beyond.

Hoʻokō ʻAna

In 2003–2004 we performed more than two hundred times and made several television appearances.

Hālau Hula 'O Wikolia (Gallery Kaua'i)

Sisters of the Islands

Wickliffe, Pepper Pike, and Akron, Ohio

Ke Poʻo
Donna "Dahmia" Komidar

Kūʻauhau

In 1983 I met Tahitian-born Hutia Tekurio Kaʻanapu and began my initiation into a variety of Polynesian dances. A year or two later, Cheryl Bell, from Marion, Indiana, began taking a group of dance students on annual trips to the Polynesian Cultural Center on Oʻahu. She also began hosting two seminars a year in Indiana and Florida, bringing many top *kumu hula* over to instruct us in the traditional way of dancing.

Our first *kumu* was Keith Awai from the Polynesian Cultural Center, who filled our lives with the culture of the islands.

I am excited and honored to have joined, at the end of 2003, a five-year *ʻūniki* class with Kumu Hula Mapuana de Silva.

Nā Lālā

We come together from the different cities to perform. I use video as a practice tool, and when we all meet, somehow it all comes together. Each spring and fall as many as two hundred of us gather in Indianapolis for hula.

Akeakamai

Hula has opened up a whole new way of expressing our love of God and others, particularly when we dance to such lovely songs as "Kanaka Wai Wai."

Manaʻo Pūlama

We have truly become a hula *ʻohana* and have shared many joys and sorrows. When our hula sister Donna Hoye choreographed "Ka Loke," in honor of her sixteen-year-old daughter Dawn's passing, she invited many of us to honor Dawn with a hula. It was a beautiful tribute and we all felt a strong bond of love, which only hula could bring.

Hoʻokō ʻAna

Recently I hosted a Polynesian Dancers' Getaway in Orlando, Florida. We celebrated with dancers from many different states who came to share the spirit of aloha through hula. Minnie Morey, from Grand Rapids, Michigan, and Margie Mitchell, from Cleveland, Ohio, helped me with the choreography. Auntie Kauʻi Brandt graciously took time out of her busy schedule to teach. Auntie's niece, Wendy, brought beautiful leis. It was such a great experience that we plan to make it an annual event.

Sisters of the Islands

Spirit of the Pacific Islands

Cincinnati, Ohio

Ke Poʻo
Francesca Anching Trego

Kūʻauhau
Born and raised in Guam, Francesca has been dancing the dances of the Pacific Islands since she was a child. She has studied hula in Tahiti and in Hawaiʻi under Nā Kumu Hula Sonny Ching, Chinky Māhoe, and Keith Awai. She has been performing professionally for a number of years.

Akeakamai
Because of her love and passion for the cultures, history, and people of the Pacific Islands, Francesca decided to share the rich diversity and beauty of the Pacific through dance. She opened her *hālau* in 2000 and trained others interested in the beauty of the hula to share the spirit of aloha. Francesca requires her dancers to hold the teachings close to their hearts and to express their feelings each time they dance, whether for an audience of thousands or for themselves.

Nā Lālā
Spirit of the Pacific Islands is a "mini-United Nations," with ethnic heritages from Hawaiʻi, Tahiti, Pohnpei, Guam, the Philippines, Peru, Russia, Germany, Mexico, and China. Spirit of the Pacific Islands continues to grow as new dancers join in sharing the beauty and grace of the hula.

Manaʻo Pūlama
One of the greatest highlights for Spirit of the Pacific Islands occurred when we were invited to perform the half-time event at the U.S. Bank Arena when the Cincinnati Cyclones hosted the Hawaiian Islanders for the indoor arena football game. Afterward, the Islanders were most gracious and shared moments and photos with the dancers. *Mahalo* Islanders!

Hoʻokō ʻAna
Spirit of the Pacific Islands performs within the Tri-States of Ohio, Indiana, and Kentucky. Each year, 2004 being the fourth year, the *hālau* and the Cure Our Kids Foundation host a full luau to raise funds for the Cincinnati Children's Hospital Cystic Fibrosis Research. In addition, we perform USO Shows for some of the veterans hospitals and nursing homes in Ohio and Kentucky. The *hālau* also offers educational presentations to ethnic events, fairs, schools, corporations, radio/television shows, and privately held companies. The *hālau* brings the full flavor of the Pacific Islands with authentic dances, dress, and music.

*S*pirit of the Pacific Islands

Aunty Malia's Hula Troupe

Ashland, Oregon, a small town nestled in a valley of pine trees and madrones

Ke Poʻo
Malia Nelson, who has been dancing since she was three years old

Kūʻauhau
Malia received the gift of hula at an early age. Her grandmother, Olga Raber, owned a tapa shop in Waikīkī, where three-year-old Malia performed for tourists. Malia's pure Hawaiian grandmother, Hattie Kaleohano, and her professional hula dancer aunties supported her dancing and encouraged her to learn about Hawaiian history and culture.

Nā Lālā
The hula troupe is an unlikely menagerie of women and girls between the ages of eleven and fifty-six. Their eclectic ethnic backgrounds are readily visible: white skin, coffee skin; long hair, short hair; stocky bodies, lithe bodies. What they have in common is a love of and commitment to hula. Many students say hula has given them a sense of grace, beauty, and confidence.

Malia's students will attest that a certain magic happens when they get together and begin dancing. As hands and hips tell the stories of the islands—celebrating a true love, catching a fish, gathering seaweed with family—the women are transformed somehow, moving as one to tell the universal and timeless tales of Hawaiʻi.

Akeakamai
Malia feels an urgency to carry on the island traditions and culture to ensure its perpetuation, as the number of pure Hawaiians is diminishing. She stresses the aloha spirit and the importance of sharing it so future generations remember the Hawaiians and what they stand for.

Malia says the most rewarding part of hula is dancing in worship to God and teaching others of His love through dance.

Manaʻo Pūlama
Malia's students trained since springtime for their second year of dancing in the local Fourth of July parade. When Malia gave them the signal, they splashed down the street like an ocean wave—some in handmade grass skirts, some in matching pareos, all draped in leis—to the loud approval of onlookers. Pulling together an entry for the parade was a lot of work, but it paid off. They won first prize.

Hoʻokō ʻAna
Soon after winning at the Fourth of July parade, the *hālau* began making shell headdresses and thirty *pāʻū* for their upcoming two-song performance at the Craterian Theatre, the region's most distinctive entertainment venue.

Aunty Malia's Hula Troupe

Noelani's Hula Studio

Montrose, a small town in northeastern Pennsylvania where people still express surprise when they first discover that hula is being taught locally

Ke Po'o

Noelani Jenkins, a native of Woodbury, New Jersey, has been studying hula since she was seven years old. Since then, wherever she has lived, Noelani has been a student or teacher of hula. Throughout her life, she has turned to hula for comfort in moments of sadness and for celebration in moments of joy.

Kū'auhau

Noelani's first teacher, Terry Johnson, instilled in her a love of hula and everything Hawaiian. Since graduating from high school, Noelani has attended hula seminars in Hawai'i and in the continental U.S with well-known *kumu*. She especially cherishes and is perhaps most grateful to Kau'i Healani Brant, who has taught her so much.

Nā Lālā

Noelani enjoys sharing her knowledge with the many wonderful people who have become her students and friends. She hopes to instill in her students a love of hula, so that it may become as special to them as it is to her.

Akeakamai

Noelani's Hula Studio emphasizes sharing all things Hawaiian: the language, dance, music, culture, and values of the aloha spirit.

Mana'o Pūlama

The *hālau* has performed at school assembly programs, cultural events, nursing homes, and other special events. Noelani appreciates the opportunity to spread aloha to the residents and visitors in the audience.

Ho'okō 'Ana

The *hālau* regularly performs at the annual 'Ohana Christmas Luau and Blueberry Festival, a Montrose community event that benefits the Susquehanna Public Library.

94

Noelani's Hula Studio

Hula Hālau Manaʻo Hawaiʻi

Based in Tennessee, our *hālau* was founded on the principles of hospitality, unity, harmony, and aloha.

Ke Poʻo

Kalei Lam, born and raised in Honolulu, spent several years in northern California performing, competing, and studying hula before relocating to Tennessee to establish this *hālau* in 1989.

Kūʻauhau

Kalei has been blessed with a unique heritage and with the influence and encouragement of Kupuna Mary Kalaʻaupa.

Nā Lālā

As our name implies, the thoughts and memories of the islands are preserved in our *hālau*. Although we are physically removed from Hawaiʻi, we remain connected, retaining the spirit of aloha and perpetuating the Hawaiian culture through instructional classes, workshops, and performances. This *hālau* is the conduit through which transplanted islanders can maintain and cultivate their heritage. It is also a way for people of all races to experience Hawaiʻi and be grafted onto the Hawaiian culture.

Akeakamai

We are separated from Hawaiʻi. We cannot see the rain against the cliffs, we cannot smell the fragrant *līpoa,* and we cannot hear the surf at Waikīkī. Being away from the islands brings a deep appreciation for and desire to share, preserve, and perpetuate the culture, so we keep the *manaʻo* in our hearts and express it in our hula. Our *pule* is that the spirit of aloha inhabits each and every hula.

Manaʻo Pūlama

It is very rewarding to experience the emotions that flow through performing the hula: the *mana* that rises up within a dancer or musician, as well as the interaction between dancer and dancer, dancer and musician, dancer and audience, and musician and audience. When the *kaona* imbedded in the lyrics is released and transfers to the motions of the dancer, the performance becomes a moving spiritual event.

Hula Hālau Mana'o Hawai'i

Hālau Hoʻola Ka Mana O Hawaiʻi

Started in 1997 in Dallas, Texas, Hālau Hoʻola Ka Mana O Hawaiʻi has expanded to San Antonio and Houston.

Kumu Hula
Frank Keliʻi Chang

Kūʻauhau
My formal training began with my parents, Frank and Moana Chang. I also tutored with Newton Kaʻanohi Hitchcock, Rebecca Hoʻopi Bodner, Sara Moanikealaonapuamakahikina Wood-Naluai, and George Ainsley Kananiakeakua Holokai. They all taught me the meaning of pride and respect and the great necessity of passing on fading family and cultural traditions of *mele* and hula.

Akeakamai
Hula has brought our families and friends closer together and has given us a sense of belonging to an ever-blending world. Hula makes our culture unique and identifiable. Not everyone knows what hula means, but the minute they see what it is, they know it comes from Hawaiʻi. My main objective is to train and tutor *haumāna* who will someday become great teachers. I have been showered with the many blessings that my teachers expect me to uphold. It is up to me to keep what I was taught pure, clean, and unadulterated.

Manaʻo Pūlama
We have been invited to participate in many cultural events here and abroad. One of the local events, "Dickens on the Strand," recreates the Victorian era in old England, with guests bedecked in old-English attire. The committee of the event learned that King Kalākaua was in England during the reign of Queen Victoria and invited us to participate. We marched in the parade with the queen of the event along with our King Kalākaua. Our *hālau* made eight *kāhili* to accompany our royal king. Two of them were fitted with crowns of royalty.

Hoʻokō ʻAna
In 1998, we were invited to participate in the King Kamehameha Hula Competition in Honolulu. In 2000, and again in 2001, we were invited to participate in the Merrie Monarch Festival in Hilo, Hawaiʻi. As a *hoʻokupu* for inviting us to the Merrie Monarch Festival, we gave Aunty Dottie Thompson, founder of the event, a Texas mountain laurel seed lei. To our delight, she used the lei for the official 2001 Merrie Monarch Festival lei motif for the T-shirts and sweaters. Our *hālau* has been the only *hālau* East of the Rocky Mountains ever to be invited to participate in this memorable event. We were so very privileged to be the first group to open the competition in the new millennium.

Hālau Hoʻola Ka Mana O Hawaiʻi

Hālau Hoʻomau I Ka Wai Ola O Hawaiʻi

Virginia

Kumu Hula

After attending his first luau in 1957, Manu Ikaika's interest in the art of Hawaiian music, hula, and other Polynesian dancing was born.

Kūʻauhau

My first *kumu hula* was the renowned musician, composer, and recording artist John Piʻilani Watkins, whom I studied with for many years. I also had the privilege of studying under the late Kumu Hula Harold Dole Mahealani (Mahina) Bailey for fourteen years.

A special *mahalo* to my father and *ʻohana*, senators Daniel K. Akaka and Daniel K. Inouye, Auntie Mercy Keola Rosa and *ʻohana*, Danny Kaleikini, Kimo Kahoano, O'Brian Eselu, Dennis Kamakahi, George Kahumoku, Cyril and Martin Pahinui, the late Darrell Lupenui, Thadius Wilson, and Kekua Fernandez, *nā alakaʻi* and *lima hana* Juanita Kealoha Cox, Kuʻuipo Domingo, Gabby Gabonia and *ʻohana*, Cynthia Kaleinani Kee, Kathy Uluwehi Knowles, Joy Hauoli Labez, Carol Takafuji and *ʻohana*, Doreen Pumehana Winkler, Carol Pohai Wong, my students, my son, Dwayne Ikaikaloa Strong, Jr., and my wife, Suzanne. You have blessed my life and encouraged me to make a difference.

Nā Lālā

Established in 2000 and blessed by Auntie Genoa Keawe, our *hālau* was named because of my belief that hula keeps us "young at heart and full of life." Auntie Nona Beamer gave me the precious *ipu heke ʻole* that belonged to her mother, Auntie Louise Beamer, not only as a blessing but also as a way to perpetuate hula and the Hawaiian culture. I try to bring a special sensitivity and *mana* to my teachings through the traditional style of hula chanting, *hula ʻolapa, hula kuʻi,* and *hula ʻauana.* In addition, I teach my *haumāna* how to play the ukulele and other ancient Hawaiian implements, as well as *nā mele o* Hawaiʻi, *ʻōlelo,* and *moʻolelo.*

Akeakamai

In honor of my two *kumu*, who left behind a legacy to *mālama*, our mission is to perpetuate traditional hula and Hawaiian culture.

Manaʻo Pūlama

My *hālau* and I have performed at the U.S. Capitol, Washington Monument, Smithsonian Institution, Barns at Wolf Trap, Kennedy Center, and Kamehameha Day Ceremony at the Statuary Hall. We also represent the Hawaiʻi Visitors and Convention Bureau and the Congressional Staff of Washington, D.C., at Hawaiian cultural events.

Hoʻokō ʻAna

In 2001, we were among a small group chosen to represent Hawaiʻi in President Bush's inaugural parade down Pennsylvania Avenue. Dressed in our *muʻumuʻu*, aloha shirts, and fragrant leis, we proudly carried a "Hawaiʻi: Land of Aloha" banner.

Hālau Hoʻomau I Ka Wai Ola O Hawaiʻi

Hālau Hula O Ka Lā

Based in Spokane, Washington, Hālau Hula O Ka Lā is part of the Northwest Hula Company, established in 2002.

Ke Poʻo

Sheri Maier, a part-Hawaiian native of Kauaʻi, attended Brigham Young University in Hawaiʻi and performed at the Polynesian Cultural Center for five years before moving to Kalispell, Montana, to pioneer the state's first hula *hālau*. She founded and taught at Paradise Productions for ten years before moving to Spokane. Today, three former *haumāna* of Paradise Productions head their own halaus in Montana.

Kūʻauhau

Sheri's line of *kumu* includes Kuulei Punua and Lovey Apana of Kauaʻi, Keith Awai and Cy Bridges of Oʻahu, and Lovey Helekahi of Maui.

Nā Lālā

We have students between the ages of four and seventy-four from Coeur d'Alene, Idaho, as well as from Cheney, Medical Lake, and Mead, Washington. Many of our *wāhine* have learned hula as children in Hawaiʻi or the continental United States and enjoy being able to continue the Hawaiian tradition while they visit or live in Spokane. We specialize in *hula kahiko*, perform Hawaiian chants, and encourage our students to visit the islands often.

Akeakamai

We are a place for people who are from Hawaiʻi or who have a connection with the islands to continue the hula and share the aloha spirit.

Manaʻo Pūlama

In 2003 we performed with Hawaiian slack key guitarists Cyril Pahinui and Patrick Landeza at the Met in Spokane. We also perform each year at First Night Spokane, the Fall Folk Festival, the Valley Fest, and other venues.

Hoʻokō ʻAna

We are the first formally organized *hālau* in Spokane. Many local colleges offer Hawaiian clubs, but members perform hula only on occasion. Our *hālau*'s name means "Hula School of Spokane." "Spokane" is Native American for "of the sun" or "people of the sun." Even when it is snowing and cold, warm smiles still radiate from our graceful hula maidens.

Hālau Hula O Ka Lā

Ka Lei Mokihana No Ke Akua

The *hālau,* whose name means "The Lei Mokihana Belonging to God," was established in Seattle, Washington, in 1996.

Nā Po'o
Mokihana Marticio-Caro and Regina Kuananiakua Shimomura

Nā Lālā
Geographically, our members come from the greater Puget Sound region. Ethnically, we are a diverse group: Hawaiian, Filipino, Chinese, Japanese, Korean, Samoan, Caucasian, and African American. We may come from different walks of life, but we come together out of our love for hula.

Akeakamai
What we learn in hula we apply to life, including our love and respect for others as well as for ourselves. We are there for guidance, advice, support, and comfort—not only in hula, but also in everyday life. Expression of our innermost feelings is a key factor for us. Hula is an outlet for us to show others how we feel. The most important thing that we have gained through our hula is the understanding that hula will always be there for us no matter where our lives take us. We may not live in Hawai'i, and some of us are not ethnically Hawaiian, but what makes us Hawaiian is the aloha that we have in our hearts and minds for the land, the people, the culture, and most of all for each other.

Mana'o Pūlama
Participating in several regional competitions has given us opportunities to meet new people and keep in touch with people from the past. Our most cherished memories come from knowing that we did our best and that we were able to share our knowledge of the hula. To see a smile on a person's face, a tear in their eye, or to receive a hug from another participant lets us know that we touched their hearts with aloha and that aloha is our hula.

Ho'okō 'Ana
We had the opportunity of a lifetime to attend the Merrie Monarch Hula Festival. The experience was unlike any other, especially for those of us who had never been to Hawai'i before. It was thrilling to watch the various *hālau* onstage in the Edith Kanaka'ole Tennis Stadium. We could feel the magnificent energy from the dancers, the audience, and the ancestors who watch over us.

Ka Lei Mokihana No Ke Akua

Mālamalama O Ka Mahina

Leavenworth, Washington, is a picturesque Bavarian-themed tourist destination village in the Pacific Northwest. Long ago it was the summer home of the Wenatchi, a tribe of the first people who were nurtured by this ancient, sacred land. The air still shimmers with their energy.

Kumu Hula

Momi Palmieri is encouraged and filled with joy when she positively impacts other people's lives. Hula is her passion.

Kūʻauhau

During my years in Hawaiʻi, I was graciously given the great gift of hula training by Kumu Hula Mapuana deSilva and her husband, Kīhei. Under the giant *kamani* tree in their Lanikai backyard, they led the way. I also learned from other hula masters, as Mapu sent me to study with those whose teachings she valued. And I learned from beloved Hawaiian musicians and righteous hula sisters along our sometimes tandem path to hula knowledge.

Nā Lālā

My mission is to teach the *mele*, dances, history, and culture of the Hawaiian Islands while providing a *puʻuhonua,* or place of refuge, for my students. In today's sensory-overloaded world, hula allows my students to expand their awareness both of the Hawaiian tradition and of themselves.

Our weekly classes are full of inclusion and *ʻohana*. It is a time of sisterhood and laughter and dance. My students are given the opportunity to grow spiritually based on the foundations of care, respect, and honor for one another. Each of my *ʻolapa*, from young children to the grown women in my *hālau*, is a delicate and beautiful flower in the garden of my life. Together we are weaving a very precious, very rare lei of aloha.

Akeakamai

The true power of the gift of hula is in the giving—passing it along to others who thirst for it as much as I do. I share my love of hula with deep aloha, great care, and honor for my *kumu* and *kūpuna*.

Hoʻokō ʻAna

Over many years I've learned to trust my training and the knowledge given to me by my *kumu*. Most of all, I've learned to trust myself. I've also learned to count on the volcano's hot breath, the soothing Malanai winds, the *pueo*'s protective call, the blessed healing rain, and the lone soaring *ʻiwa*. I am inspired by all of this and more.

Mālamalama O Ka Mahina

Hālau Hula ʻO Maile Lei

Milwaukee, Wisconsin

Ke Poʻo
Anita Bradley

Kūʻauhau
We are blessed because we've been able to learn from many well-known *kumu* throughout the years. Although many of us learned hula as little girls from our local *kumu*, the real fun began when we attended a seminar led by Keith Awai. Keith is the first *kumu* from Hawaiʻi to come to Indiana to teach at a weekend seminar that is now held twice a year.

Since then, we have learned various styles and songs from Ray Fonseca, Chinky Māhoe, Sonny Ching, Vicky Holt Takamine, Leimomi Ho, Kealiʻi Reichel, Ellen Gay Dela Rosa, Kaulana Kasparovitch, Leialoha Lim Amina, Leinaʻala Heine, and Moon Kauakahi.

Nā Lālā
As we learn new dances, we focus not only on getting the motions correctly but also on understanding what the songs are about. We believe this is important so that we are able to bring out the spirit from within and interpret the dance through our movements. We love learning about the history of hula and teaching this and other Hawaiian traditions to our younger members.

Akeakamai
It is our belief that one doesn't have to be born Hawaiian to appreciate the artistry of hula. Hula comes from the heart. If we feel it on the inside, it will show in the beauty and grace of our performance.

Manaʻo Pūlama
Several years ago, Kumu Hula Chinky Māhoe asked us to perform with the Mākaha Sons, who were coming to our Indiana seminar to put on a concert. We were not only honored but absolutely thrilled at the opportunity. This excitement would not end that night, as we would later perform with the Mākaha Sons at three of their mainland concerts.

One of our annual performances is at the local Holiday Folk Fair, which showcases groups representing different cultures from around the world. Many of our members perform in this three-day event, and we always look forward to keeping the tradition alive.

Hoʻokō ʻAna
We are not just hula sisters, but friends. We enjoy celebrating holidays and other life events together. Whenever we visit Hawaiʻi, we love seeing local bands and dancers perform hula to live music. A recent group trip to Hawaiʻi was to attend the wedding of one of our hula sisters. At the ceremony we danced with Genoa Keawe and Dennis Kamakahi! We have been richly blessed.

Hālau Hula 'O Maile Lei

International

Hālau Hula ʻO Walea

Toronto, Ontario, Canada

Ke Poʻo
Joy Walea Corpuz

Kūʻauhau
My *kumu* was Renee Makamae Cruz, noted as the first to have brought the Hula to Toronto, and arguably, to Canada. Under her direction, I studied hula for thirteen years.

Akeakamai
In 1994, Auntie Renee stepped down as *kumu hula* and passed the *hālau* onto her two *alakaʻi*: Tina Kuʻuiwa Lacho-Carr, and me, Joy Walea Corpuz. Iwa and I accepted this task with the greatest honor and humility. The Iwalea Dance Company was born—Iwalea being the combination of our Hawaiian names. As more and more *haumāna* walked through the doors, yearning to learn the hula, we shared our limited knowledge of the art. Auntie Renee taught us that not all wisdom is found in one *hālau*, and like her, we strongly encouraged our *haumāna* to attend workshops offered by great hula masters, including Chinky Māhoe, Sonny Ching, Olana Ai, and Aloha Dalire. When Iwa got married and moved to Japan, I took over the direction of the *hālau* and renamed it Hālau Hula ʻO Walea. Now with over eighty *haumāna*, we continue the tradition of spreading our love of the hula.

Manaʻo Pūlama
My most vivid memory is of the Ka Hula Leʻa competition on the Big Island of Hawaiʻi in August 2002. I recall stepping onto the stage and noticing the dozens of fans who had traveled thousands of miles to cheer our *hālau* on. There they sat, with their Canadian flags waving ferociously, donned in our *hālau* T-shirts, their faces shining with the utmost pride and joy.

Hoʻokō ʻAna
In our final year together, Iwa and I returned to Hawaiʻi for the King Kamehameha Hula Competition to represent Canada, but more important, to share our love for hula, a love that comes all the way from the land of snow. Iwa and I took our *haumāna* out by the ocean for *hoʻoponopono* the night before the first day's competition, to let go of all the *pilikia*, so they could dance in the purest spirit of aloha. After the tears and embraces, the girls stood on the rocks and chanted their *oli* overlooking the ocean. As their voices resonated across the water, the waves crashed against the stones and the tropical wind whipped through the air. I knew that God, in His awesome splendor, was blessing our *haumāna* for what was to come.

Halau Hula 'O Walea

Paul Latta Dancers (Hula Hālau Ma'ema'ekapuaokahala)

North Surrey, British Columbia, Canada

Ke Po'o

In the deep South Pacific, Paul Tavai-Latta grew up knowing the hula as a very modern dance, nothing like its Polynesian cousins and nothing like he would later come to know. In the 1960s, hula had been commercialized: *u'ehe* were called "puffs," *pū'ili* were painted fluorescent pink, a great hula was "Lovely Hula Hands," plastic leis adorned blue tapa *mu'umu'u,* and the Kodak Hula Show was considered authentic.

Paul, who had danced and performed since the age of three, began producing small shows and teaching neighborhood children when he was eleven. As an adult, he became a teacher and then a student. He learned hula the hard way—backwards. Day after day he returned to his Polynesian roots, sympathetic to the desires of the modern audience and what it wanted to see, yet knowing in his heart that it was not what he wanted. And what he wanted was what he eventually found: what he had expected the hula to be, what he missed, what made him homesick for his days as a child—the proud dances he came to know as Polynesian.

Kū'auhau

Kalani Po'omihalani taught me about the honesty and native simplicity of old hula. I watched my friend Paulette dance nightly with Tavana, whose perfect blend of authentic dance productions and showmanship I admired. Uncle George Na'ope encouraged me to keep dancing all Polynesian dances while studying a form of hula that was becoming popular in the '70s—*kahiko*.

Nā Lālā

I come from an era that did not have the hula we know today. My Hawai'i and hula are from a time that seemed to deny its roots, when the new outweighed the old and the past was something to forget.

Hula has now come full circle with its past, and it is still growing in every new direction, as any art form does. I teach my students to research the past, encouraging them to find what I found, go as far back as they can, learn the true basics, study the geography and culture, and learn hula steps never used when I was growing up.

After thirty-five years I, too, have come full circle. I have brought together my two loves, creating the most authentic, indigenous dances of old and new Polynesia, and showcasing them in the most entertaining way I know how.

Akeakamai

Find the "Polynesian" in your hula!

Paul Latta Dancers (Hula Hālau Ma'ema'ekapuaokahala)

Hālau Hula O Mānoa

Paris

Kumu Hula

Sandra Kilohana Silve, an art historian, combines art and hula in her teaching. She believes that dancing hula is like painting pictures in space with one's entire being.

Kūʻauhau

Growing up in Mānoa, I had the privilege of studying with Mama Bishop. I've also been a long-distance student of Ellen Castillo, whose patient instruction I return to each year. My *kumu* have taught me that "*aʻohe pau ka ʻike i ka hālau hoʻokahi*" (all knowledge is not taught in the same school).

Our *hālau* has received beautiful choreographies from such gifted *kumu hula* as Uncle George Holokai, Coline Aiu, Lika Moon, and Kilohana Sharkey. We have also received the *kōkua* of language experts Puakea Nogelmeier, Carol Silva, and Ipolani Vaughan. Milton Keʻaulana Holt has been a tremendous help with our choreography, translation, and research projects.

Nā Lālā

Our *hālau* functions like a large extended family. Never bigger than thirty or forty members, we are educating a European audience about Hawaiʻi's history and rich heritage.

I share diverse hula styles with my *haumāna*, emphasizing rigorous training and an understanding of the islands' history. There are many chants and dances I won't teach until my *haumāna* have been in the *hālau* for several years and acquired background knowledge in Hawaiian traditions.

We also learn about Hawaiian culture. I often return from Honolulu with boxes of ti leaves, rare in Paris, to teach my *haumāna* to make ti-leaf skirts. We treasure and *mālama* the leaves for weeks in the refrigerator. We've even disassembled the skirts, washed the leaves, and made *laulau*! We now grow ti plants between the radiator and French antiques.

Manaʻo Pūlama

Several years ago, we performed with Hawaiian choral group Nā Leo Kuhoʻokahi at the Conservatoire Serge Rachmaninoff. American artist Kathy Burke captured the performance in her sketchbook. Her creation marked the beginning of an exciting project. A group of artists has since met with us regularly to portray diverse elements of Hawaiian legends, traditions, and chants, and hula gestures and movements. Our collaborative result will be featured in an exhibition in 2005.

Hoʻokō ʻAna

Hawaiian vocabulary for *mele* we perform is translated into French and put into a Parisian context. Long discussions about masculine/feminine articles preceding hula vocabulary have resulted in setting the precedent for French publications on the subject.

Hālau Hula O Mānoa

Keiki O Ke Makani

Hohenfels, Germany

Ke Po'o
Gabriele Kalehua Streuer

Kū'auhau

I studied with Laelae, who also performed my wedding ceremony in Hawai'i and who graciously invited me to her house, where I first learned everything I could about the beautiful hula.

I saw my first hula when my boyfriend and I got married in Hawai'i. When I watched the beautiful hula dancers, my heart was pounding and I felt a happiness that I had never felt before. As I sat there watching them, I felt their dance touch my heart and soul, and I knew that moment would change my life forever. I was at the time an employee at a bank, constantly looking for a new profession that would fill my heart with love. It drove me to despair not knowing what to do. Watching the dancers, I knew, deep within, that hula was the answer to what was missing from my life. When we got home to Germany, I practiced what I had been taught and absorbed everything I could read about Hawai'i and her culture. I am so thankful to the angels who guided me to Hawai'i to find my new profession and many cherished friends.

Akeakamai

Through hula we express the love we feel and the culture we have learned, and we work to make the world a little better through music and dance.

Mana'o Pūlama

I once performed for Genoa Keawe. I had joined Laelae's *hālau,* and one night we went to listen to the magical voice of Auntie Genoa. Laelae told her I was a student and she invited me to dance. There I was in Hawai'i, dancing by the sea and watching the beauty of a red sunset. It filled my soul with an indescribable happiness.

Ho'okō 'Ana

I recently organized a luau in Germany with all of the proceeds going to *Kindernothilfe,* an organization supporting underprivileged children throughout the world. It is our way of giving back that which has brought so much joy, happiness, and love to our lives. I wrote a book in German titled *Hula, Angel and Hawai'i,* which tells about my wonderful experiences and shares what I have learned about the hula and the culture of Hawai'i.

Keiki O Ke Makani

Hālau Hula ʻO Mehanaokalā

Japan

Kumu Hula

Kuʻuleinani Hashimoto has been teaching hula in Japan since 1979 and has translated the Hawaiian textbook *Ka Lei Haʻaheo* into Japanese.

Kūʻauhau

My ballet teacher taught hula, and I started dancing as a *keiki*. In 1971, I began studying hula in Hawaiʻi. Nā Kumu Hula Luka and Louise Kaleiki of the esteemed ʻIlima Hula Studio taught me Tahitian, Maori, Samoan knife

dancing, and hula. Since studying with Kumu Hula Noenoelani Zuttermeister (Aunty Noe) in 1992, I have continued to work hard and learn from Sam Pua Haʻaheo, who taught Aunty Noe's mother, Aunty Kauʻi Zuttermeister.

Nā Lālā

My *hālau* dances in the style of Aunty Noe, who taught me how to *oli*, *hoʻopaʻa*, and dance *hula kahiko* and *hula kuʻi*.

Akeakamai

Although I am not from Hawaiʻi, I will always work hard and do my best to represent the Hawaiian culture. I am so honored to be able to share the wonderful heritage of the Hawaiian people with my students and the audiences in Japan.

Hoʻokō ʻAna

In 1988, I entered the King Kamehameha Hula Competition to better understand the meaning of hula. The challenge of *hula kahiko* made me realize how much more I needed to learn about the Hawaiian culture and dance. This desire to learn more and

become a better teacher for my students led me to the University of Hawaiʻi, where I have studied the Hawaiian language for the past five years.

Hālau Hula ʻO Mehanaokalā

Hoaloha Hula Studio

Japan

Ke Po'o
Ayako Murata

Kū'auhau

My background was in modern dance, jazz, and various ethnic dances. I became a professional dancer and eventually organized a dance school for ballet and jazz. But it was not enough, for I still yearned to dance the hula. So I followed my heart and started studying hula under Noenoelani Zuttermeister. In 1983, I became an instructor with Hālau Hula 'O Mehanaokalā. Through the years, I also continue to seek guidance from TeHani Kealamailani Gonzado. I have great respect for her wisdom, interpretation, and beautiful hula.

Akeakamai

I have always felt that receiving knowledge never ends and comes from many sources. I will continue to study the Hawaiian history, culture, and traditions so that I may properly give back to my students. I believe that traditional culture must be honored and respected. In my hula studio, I instill this honor and respect within my students' hearts and minds through every word I say and every movement I teach.

Ho'okō 'Ana

When I saw the hula for the very first time, I felt it was a beautiful, feminine expression. Seeing the happiness beaming on the dancers' faces touched my heart with joy. I was filled with longing to learn the hula. My dream finally came true in 1997 when I opened my own hula school, Hoaloha Hula Studio. In the beginning, it was not easy. I learned that, unlike ballet and jazz dancing, the art of hula is more expressive of the feelings that come not only from the words of the song but also from deep within your heart. It is like telling a story with every hand movement as you convey a certain thought or feeling. I also felt that it was impossible to simply dance to the music without first learning the background of the song, along with the history and culture of the islands. Today, that is paramount in my own dancing and in my teaching.

We entered and took first place in the King Kamehameha Hula Competition in 2000 and second in 2002 here in Japan, and were honored to compete in Hawai'i in 2001, where we placed fourth. Competition is a wonderful opportunity for students to gain invaluable knowledge and learn of the strict dedication and discipline involved while receiving much enjoyment.

Hoaloha Hula Studio

Hula Hālau O Kaleihua

Japan

Ke Poʻo
Lehua Tomoko

Kūʻauhau
My first encounter with hula dates back to 1970. Since then I have come to appreciate and love everything connected to the islands. I deeply respect Hawaiʻi's people, culture, and history. Hula and Hawaiian music have moved me, touched my soul, and become an inseparable part of my life.

During my travels to Hawaiʻi, I have had the pleasure of meeting many respected *kumu hula* and beautiful Hawaiian people. They have graced me with their kindness, wisdom, gentleness, and warmth. They have also taught me the importance of strictness in teaching.

Nā Lālā
I will study the Hawaiian culture and its traditions for the rest of my life. This will enable me to carefully hand down to my students that which the Hawaiian people have nurtured and graciously shared with me—the hula. Its wonderful music and creative beauty have brought eternal happiness not only to my *hālau*, but also to countless people living in Japan.

Akeakamai
My mentors have shown me that even sadness in life can make a positive difference in the portrayal of the music and dance. To me, this is part of what makes up the beauty of hula.

Hula Hālau O Kaleihua

Hula Hālau O Leilani

Formed in 1996 in Chigasaki, Japan, we now have several branches and over 400 students.

Ke Poʻo
Mihoko Ogawa

Kūʻauhau
I first began studying hula in Japan with Lehua Nani Satake. In Hawaiʻi, I had the opportunity to meet OʻBrian Eselu. I was very impressed with the strength of his *kāne* dancers and the beauty of his *wāhine* dancers, especially Tracie Lopes, formerly Tracie Farias, Miss Aloha Hula in 1996. Tracie's influence on OʻBrian's *wāhine* dancers inspired me to study with them. She and her husband, Keawe Lopes, eventually became my advisors. They taught me about hula and Hawaiian traditions and have assisted me in everything from competitions to music and costumes. I feel most honored to have their continued *kōkua*.

Nā Lālā
I began to teach hula in Japan to my friends, and shortly thereafter, more and more students came to me. Recently I saw that many *keiki* were interested in the hula and I began teaching them too. Most *keiki* in Japan are taught only a limited number of songs and perform only occasionally. I try to instill more depth and want them to have pride in learning the hula.

Akeakamai
I teach in a different way from other Japanese *hālau,* desiring to keep a more Hawaiian style to our dancing, with the motions and smoothness of the dance. I feel it is important to emphasize the meaning of the song and individual expressions of the dancers. I want my *keiki haumāna* to gain appreciation through participating in the many events in Hawaiʻi and to learn firsthand the beauty of the Hawaiian culture. My goal is to inspire them as I was inspired. I feel a responsibility to pass on all that I have learned in the same spirit of sharing and to take care to preserve the integrity of the Hawaiian culture.

Manaʻo Pūlama
In 2000, our *wāhine* group was honored to perform for exhibition at the Merrie Monarch Hula Festival on the Big Island.

Hoʻokō ʻAna
One of our *hālau*'s greatest dreams came true in 2001 when we were invited to Honolulu to participate in the Hula ʻOni E Keiki Hula Festival. We were the first *hālau* from Japan to be invited to a *keiki* competition. It was a proud and very happy moment when our eight-year-old dancer Rukako Takahashi won third place in the Miss Hula ʻOni E category.

Hula Hālau O Leilani

Hula Pō'ai Nālei

Based in Kichijoji, Japan, we have been performing since 1992, a time when a handful of hula studios were beginning to appear only in much larger cities such as Osaka and Nagoya. Hawaiian music was the beginning of hula's popularity in Japan. Although records show that hula made its first appearance during the Taisho era (1912–1926), the big Hawaiian boom was accompanied by the sound of the steel guitar. By the end of World War II, Japanese people were wildly enthusiastic about Hawaiian music.

Ke Po'o

Naleili'ili'i Ito teaches classes in her studio and has also been asked to give hula lessons at local community and culture centers.

Nā Lālā

Our *haumāna* have come together from diverse backgrounds. Some are interested in the dances of different countries; others feel that dance will improve their health. However, everyone is captivated with the beauty of Hawai'i and the graceful charms and elegant gestures of the hula. Our lives have been enriched and deepened by learning the meaning of hula movements, as well as the language, history, geography, customs, myths, and legends of old Hawai'i. We have also enjoyed making leis, crafts, and intricate costumes.

A few times each year, we invite *kumu* from Hawai'i to Japan and hold workshops. I encourage my *haumāna* to absorb the positive qualities of each *kumu* and understand that each *hālau* has a unique way of dancing hula.

Akeakamai

Even if our technique does not come close to that of the gracious Hawaiian people, we are honored to be dancing hula with an understanding of its diverse background. I hope to share this knowledge with my *haumāna* and to continue dancing with an open, generous spirit.

Mana'o Pūlama

Our *hālau* looks forward to participating in the annual *ho'olaule'a* and *hō'ike* celebrations. We also take part in voluntary activities, such as visiting retirement homes and hospices on Respect-for-the-Aged Day to perform dances and bring smiles to many faces. My *haumāna* also enjoy dancing in annual summer and autumn festivals in Kichijoji.

Ho'okō 'Ana

It fills me with joy to watch children who have learned hula grow up and spread their wings. There is nothing more delightful than seeing ties develop and strengthen among people who dance hula, while their lives become enriched as a result.

Hula Pōʻai Nālei

Nā Lei O Pōpōhau

Based in Japan, we have several studios and have performed for more than a decade.

Ke Poʻo

Keiko Terabe, who has danced since she was five years old, credits her musical parents for opening the path that led to her career as a hula teacher. She has devoted her life to learning and teaching hula and considers herself to be one of Japan's finest in the field.

Kūʻauhau

Keiko has studied hula in Hawaiʻi under the tutelage of Kumu Hula Tony Conjugacion.

Nā Lālā

We maintain a family closeness, which we feel is imperative to create a unified look when performing or competing. We always encourage each other to be the best that we can be.

Akeakamai

Our *hālau* is for people who enjoy sharing, dancing, and being part of a family. Most important, it is for those who love, respect, and honor hula, Hawaiʻi, and its culture.

Manaʻo Pūlama

For the past four years, we have entered many hula competitions, including the King Kamehameha Hula Competition and Japan/Kauaʻi Mokihana Festivals.

Hoʻokō ʻAna

In April 2003, we opened new studios in Kamakura and Kanagawa, Japan. Five months later, we held our tenth anniversary Hoʻike. To memorialize this wonderful occasion, we met regularly to create the Nā Lei o Pōpōhau *hālau* quilt. This quilt features the *pōpōhau,* a hydrangea renowned in Kamakura, Japan.

Nā Lei O Pōpōhau

Nā Mamo O Kaleinani

Gotanda, Tokyo, Japan

Ke Po'o

Kaleinanikauikawekiu Seiko Okamoto is not in a hurry to obtain the title of *kumu hula*. She finds it more important to learn everything she can before going through the process of a formal *'ūniki*. She knows that someday her dream of becoming a *kumu hula* will become a reality. Until then, she shares the knowledge that has been given to her with much honor and respect.

Kū'auhau

Although it is difficult for those living abroad to obtain instruction in the art of hula, Kaleinani has studied under the direction of Kumu Hula Aloha Dalire during Kumu Aloha's visits to Japan for the past ten years. Kaleinani relies heavily on Kumu Aloha to quench her thirst and desire for greater knowledge of the dance, the culture, and the history of Hawai'i.

Nā Lālā

In 1998, Kaleinani opened her *hālau* in Gotanda, Tokyo, Japan. To preserve the Hawaiian culture and its protocol, she encourages her students to take classes with Kumu Aloha or her daughter, Keola Dalire, whenever they visit Japan.

Mana'o Pūlama

Nā Mamo o Kaleinani enjoyed traveling to O'ahu, Hawai'i, to enter the World Invitational Hula Festival in 2002 and the King Kamehameha Hula Competition in 2003.

Ho'okō 'Ana

With the support of Kumu Aloha, who encouraged Kaleinani to use competition as a tool to gain greater knowledge and for her students to become better dancers, Nā Mamo O Kaleinani began entering hula competitions in 2001. They have since won more than twelve awards in *hula 'auana* and *hula kahiko*. They have also traveled the world and entered competitions in Tokyo, Guam, California, and Las Vegas.

Nā Mamo O Kaleinani

Hālau Hula Fa'arere 'Ike

Mexico

Ke Po'o
Karina Constantini Fascinetto

Alaka'i
Jocelyn Garcia Badillo

Nā Lālā
Our *hālau* began in 1998 as part of the National System for the Integral Development of the Family's cultural activities. We searched for a name based on our ideas of what life is all about. Seeking an answer from Hawaiian literature, we found an article about the meaning of aloha and learned that the word *'ike* means "knowledge, thoughts, and perception."

We interpret "Fa'arere 'Ike" to mean "Remember that the world is what we think it is." With this idea we emphasize the strength of our minds and our hearts' desires. For every idea, thought, or wish, we accomplish changes in all that surrounds us. This involves responsibility and conscious-ness in our acts, as what we do in life affects everything and everyone around us. Our *hālau* believes that if we work together toward a common goal, we can change the world. We can live in peace and joy.

Young students form the greater part of our *hālau*. We strive to fill their lives with knowledge of the Hawaiian culture, and stress the philosophy of aloha. We work to preserve and pass on knowledge as it was taught. We also emphasize the importance of supporting each other with respect and dedication.

Akeakamai
Each one of us is part of the wondrous universe. Many people have already walked a long way and possess great wisdom. Others are new souls seeking guidance, knowledge, and answers to their questions. This is why our motto is *"Kama hele nei e hana na'auao,"* or "The child must go forward to seek the knowledge."

Hālau Hula Fa'arere 'Ike

Hālau Hula ʻO Maiʻana

Netherlands

Ke Poʻo
Conchita Joenoes

Nā Lālā
Most of the dancers in our *hālau* are Dutch-Indonesians. Born in the Netherlands and raised with a mixture of Indonesian and European influences, we often feel lost, without a homeland with a culture of its own. (Our ancestors are from Indonesia, a group of islands in Southeast Asia that became a melting pot of Dutch, Portuguese, Chinese, and other cultures throughout colonial times. In the late 1950s, for a variety of reasons, many Dutch-Indonesians moved to the Netherlands and the United States.) We are not Dutch, but neither are we Indonesian. In the Netherlands, we are much too Asian; in Indonesia, we are much too European. But when dancing hula and visiting Hawaiʻi, we feel that we fit in and are in place, exactly where we belong. We feel one with the people, one with the land, and one with the culture. Maybe we feel this bond because the Indonesian people were among the first to travel to and later inhabit Polynesia. Perhaps it's that the food and strong family bonds of Hawaiʻi are so similar to our own. Or it might be because we grew up with Hawaiian music and dancing, which were always very popular in the Dutch-Indonesian community

Akeakamai
Dancing hula allows us to express our feelings, spread our aloha in Europe, and connect with the culture, the spirit, and the emotions of the land we call home—Hawaiʻi.

Manaʻo Pūlama
At the 1997 World Invitational Hula Festival E Hoʻi Mai I Ka Piko Hula, we were invited onstage to explain why we feel so connected to Hawaiʻi and what makes us experience the Hawaiian culture as part of our own. On that stage at the Waikīkī Shell, we felt so much love from and unity with the Hawaiian audience that the answer was quite simple: We are Hawaiian at heart.

Hālau Hula ‘O Mai‘ana

Glossary

A

'a'ali'i – native shrub or tree with narrow leaves, small flowers, and a yellow, red, or brown papery fruit capsule.

ahi – fire, match, lightning.

'āina – land, earth.

akeakamai – lover of wisdom, philosopher.

akua – god, goddess, spirit, ghost.

alaka'i – to lead, guide, direct; leader, guide.

alaka'i hula – hula leader.

ali'i – chief, chiefess.

aloha – love, affection, compassion, greeting.

āna – his, her, hers.

ānuenue – rainbow.

a'o – instruction, teaching.

auē, auwē – Oh dear! Alas!

'aumakua, 'aumākua (pl.) – family or personal god, deified ancestor who might assume the shape of an animal or other natural form.

H

ha'a – dance with bent knees; dancing; called hula after mid 1800s.

ha'aheo – proud, haughty.

haku – to compose, invent, put in order, arrange; to braid, as a lei, or plait, as feathers.

haku mele – poet, composer; to compose song or chant; those that speak in proverbs.

haku o ke mele, owner of the chant, the one for whom a chant was composed rather than the composer.

hālau – long house, as for canoes or hula instruction; meeting house.

halelū – psalm, in the Bible; to sing psalms.

hana – work, service; to create, perform.

hānai – foster child, adopted child; to raise, nourish.

hano – noble, honored.

haole – Caucasian; formerly, any foreigner; foreign, introduced.

hapa haole – part-white person; part white and part Hawaiian, as an individual or phenomenon.

hau – lowland tree.

haumana, haumāna (pl.) – student, disciple.

heiau – pre-Christian place of worship.

hele – to go, come, walk; to move.

Hi'iaka – sister of Pele, the fire goodess.

hoaloha – friend. *Lit.*, beloved companion.

hō'ike – to show, exhibit.

Hōkūle'a – modern-day canoe whose voyages follow ancient Polynesian routes; named after a zenith star above Hawai'i.

honi – to kiss; a kiss; formerly, to touch noses on the side in greeting.

honua – land, earth, world; background, as of quilt designs; basic at the foundation, fundamental.

ho'okahi – one, alone; to make one, unite.

ho'okō 'ana – performance, accomplishment; achievement.

ho'okupu – ceremonial gift giving to a chief as a sign of honor and respect.

ho'olaule'a – celebration, festival.

ho'omau – to continue, keep on, persist, renew, perpetuate, persevere, last.

ho'opa'a – drummer and hula chanter (the memorizer).

ho'oponopono – family conferences in which relationships are set right through prayer, discussion, confession, repentance, and mutual restitution and forgiveness.

hula 'auana – informal hula without ceremony or offering.

hula kahiko – ancient hula.

I

'ia – particle marking passive/imperative, sometimes written as a part of modified words.

'ike – to see, know, feel, recognize; knowledge, awareness.

'ilima – delicate yellow, orange, greenish, or red flower used for leis.

inoa – name, term, title.

ipu heke – gourd drum with a top section.

ipu heke 'ole – gourd drum without a top section.

'iwa – frigate or man-of-war bird; also used figuratively for a handsome person.

K

ka – definite singular article replaced by *ke* before words beginning with *a, e, o*, and *k*, and before some words beginning with the glottal stop *p*.

kahiko – ancient.

kāhili – feather standard, symbolic of royalty, segment of a rainbow standing like a shaft (also a sign of royalty).

kahu – honored attendant, guardian.

kahuna, kāhuna (pl.) – priest, sorcerer, magician, wizard, minister, expert in any profession (whether male or female).

kamali'i – children.

kanaka – person, individual, party, mankind, population.

kanaka maoli – native Hawaiian people.

kāne – male, husband, male sweetheart, man; brother-in-law of a woman.

kaona – hidden meaning, as in Hawaiian poetry; concealed reference, as to a person, thing, or place; words with double meanings.

kapu – taboo, prohibition; sacred.

ka'u – my, mine.

ke – definite article, same as *ka*, often translated "the."

ke'ena – studio or place to gather.

kēia – this, this person, this thing.

keiki – child, offspring, descendant.

kini – multitude or many.

kōkua – help, assistance, associate, deputy, helper.

kolohe – mischievous, naughty.

komo – to enter, go into, join, as a class or organization.

kū'auhau – genealogy, lineage.

ku'i – to pound, punch, strike, box, hit, or hammer.

kuleana – right, privilege, concern, responsibility.

kumu – bottom, base, foundation; basic; hereditary, fundamental; teacher, tutor.

kumu alaka'i – leading teacher; exemplary teacher, pattern, or example.

kumu hula – hula teacher.

kumulipo – origin, genesis, source of life, mystery.

kūpe'e – bracelet, anklet.

kupuna, kūpuna (pl.) – grandparent, ancestor, relative or close friend of the grandparent's generation.

L

lā – sun, sun heat; sunny, solar.

lāhui – nation, race, tribe.

lākou – they, them (more than two).

lālā – branch, limb, bough, coconut frond.

lani – sky, heaven, royal.

lauhala – leaves of the pandanus tree, used in weaving.

le'a – joy, pleasure, happiness, merriment.

lehua – flower of the *'ōhia* tree. Also the tree itself.

lei – garland, wreath; necklace of flowers, leaves, shells, ivory, feathers, or paper, given as a symbol of affection; beads; any ornament worn around the head or neck.

leo – voice, tone, tune, melody, sound, command, advice, syllable, plea, verbal message; to speak, make a sound.

liko – leaf bud.

Līloa – name of an elderly chief, father of 'Umi.

lima – arm, hand; sleeve, finger.

līpoa – brown seaweed with a unique aroma and flavor.

loa – distance, length, height; very, very much, too, excessive, most.

loea – skill, ingenuity, cleverness; expert.

Lohi'au – a chief of Kaua'i who was the center of a conflict between Pele and her sister Hi'iaka.

loke – rose.

M

mahalo – thanks, admiration.

maha'oi – rude, brazen, bold.

mahina – moon.

mai – directional part., towards the speaker, this way.

maka – eye, eye of a needle.

malama – light, month, moon.

mālama – to take care of, attend, protect, care for.

Malanai – name of a gentle breeze.

mamo – Hawaiian honeycreeper; safflower; sergeant fish; descendant.

mana – supernatural or divine power.

mana'o – thought, idea, belief, opinion, desire, want.

mana'o pūlama – cherished memories.

manawa – period of time; seat of emotions.

manuahi – gratis, gratuitous, free of charge.

mele – song, anthem, or chant of any kind; poem, poetry.

mohala – unfolded, as flower petals opening up, spread.

mokihana – native tree (*Pelea anisata*), found only on Kaua'i, belonging to the citrus family.

mo'olelo – story, tale, myth, history, tradition, literature, legend, journal, log, yarn, fable, essay, chronicle, record, article.

mu'umu'u – woman's underslip or chemise; a loose gown, so called because formerly the yoke was omitted, and sometimes the sleeves were short.

N

na – by, for, belonging to.

nā – plural definite article.

na'au – gut; mind, heart, affections; temper, feelings.

na'auao – learned, wise; knowledge.

nahenahe – soft, sweet, melodious, as music, or a gentle voice.

nani – beauty, glory, splendor.

no – of, for, because of, belonging to, honoring, behalf of, honoring, to, for, from, resulting from, concerning, about.

no'eau – clever, skillful, wise, talented.

nui – large, great, many, much.

O

o – of

'oe – you (singular), thou.

'ohana – family.

'ola – life, health, well-being, living, livelihood, salutation.

'ōlapa – dancer, as contrasted with the chanter or *ho'opa'a* (memorizer); now, any dance accompanied by chanting and drumming on a gourd drum.

'ole – not, without.

'ōlelo – language, speech, word; talk, tell.

'ōlelo no'eau – wise sayings.

oli – chant that was not danced to, especially with prolonged phrases chanted in one breath, often with a trill (*'i'i*) at the end of each phrase; to chant thus.

'onipa'a – steadfast.

'ōpio – youth.

'ōpiopio – young, juvenile, immature.

P

pahu – drum.

pakalana – Chinese violet, a plant with yellow-green flowers.

pala'ā – lace fern.

palapalai – native fern; one of the plants placed on the altar to Laka, goddess of hula.

papa – foundation.

pau – finished, ended.

pā'ū – woman's skirt, sarong, skirt worn by women horseback riders.

Pele – goddess of fire.

pīkake – small, very fragrant white flower used in leis.

piko – navel.

pilikia – trouble of any kind, great or small.

pō'ai – circle; group, as of friends.

pono – goodness, right, uprightness, morality; beneficial.

po'o – leader, director.

pōpōhau – hydrangea.

pua – flower, blossom, tassel and stem of sugar cane; to bloom, blossom.

pua kenikeni – shrub with long, fragrant white flowers, changing to orange, used in leis.

pueo – Hawaiian short-eared owl, regarded often as a benevolent *'aumakua*.

pū'ili – bamboo rattles.

pūlama – torch; to cherish.

pule – prayer.

punahele – a favorite or pet.

pu'uhonua – place of refuge, sanctuary.

pu'uwai – heart.

U

ua – rain, to rain, rainy; indicator of the dual number in first and third persons of pronouns and poss. only (*kāua, māua, lāua*).

'uehe – hula step; one foot is lifted with weight shifting to opposite hip as the foot is lowered; both knees are then pushed forward by the quick raising of the heels, with continued swaying of the hips from side to side (a difficult step); to do this step.

'uhane – soul, spirit, ghost; dirge or song of lamentation; spiritual.

'uhane kia'i – guardian spirit.

'ulī'ulī – gourd rattle, containing seeds with colored feathers at the top, used for the *hula 'ulī'ulī* (at one time there were no feathers); to rattle.

'ūniki – graduation exercise.

W

wā – at the time of.

wahine, wāhine (pl.) – woman, wife; sister-in-law, female cousin-in-law of a man.

walea – adept; to do effortlessly.

wau – I.

wela – hot, burned; heat, temperature.